Healing and Shifa

From Quran and Sunnah

By: IqraSense

This page is intentionally left blank.

﴿وَنُنَزِّلُ مِنَ الْقُرْآنِ مَا هُوَ شِفَاءٌ وَرَحْمَةٌ لِّلْمُؤْمِنِينَ﴾

And We send down of the Quran that which is a healing and a mercy to those who believe... (Quran, Surah Al-Israa, 17:82)

﴿وَإِذَا مَرِضْتُ فَهُوَ يَشْفِينِ﴾

And when I am ill, it is [God] who cures me" (Quran, Surah ash-Shu`ara, 26:80) (A supplication of Prophet Abraham [a.s.]).

اللَّهُمَّ أَذْهِبْ الْبَأْسَ رَبَّ النَّاسِ ، وَاشْفِ أَنْتَ الشَّافِي ، لَا شِفَاءَ إِلَّا شِفَاؤُكَ شِفَاءً لَا يُغَادِرُ سَقَمًا

"O Allah, Lord of mankind! It is You Who removes suffering. You are the Healer, and none can heal but You. I beg You to bring about healing that leaves behind no ailment."

Source: Saheeh Al-Bukhari, Hadith No. 5675. & Saheeh Muslim, Hadith No. 2191.

Printed in the United States of America

ISBN: **1484977416**
ISBN-13:   **978-1484977415**

Important

Information is this book provides guidance based on Islamic teachings as mentioned in Quran, Sunnah of the prophet (sallallahu alaihi wasallam) and interpretation of these teachings by various Islamic scholars. The authors of this book do not provide their own opinions on such issues.

Information is this book is NOT intended or implied to be medical advice, diagnosis, or treatment. Those should only be sought from your physician, appropriate health care provider or Islamic scholars that are knowledgeable in applying Ruqyah or Islamic spiritual treatment.

This information is only provided as an information resource and is NOT to be relied on for diagnostic and treatment purposes. It is NOT intended as patient education, and NOT a substitute for professional diagnosis and treatment and does NOT establish a patient physician relationship.

The publishers and authors expressly disclaim any responsibility, and shall have NO liability for any loss, injury, damage, or other liability whatsoever suffered as a result of your reliance on or use of the information in this book.

For any observed errors, please report them by writing to admin@IqraSense.com

This page is intentionally left blank.

TABLE OF CONTENTS

PART I – PRINCIPLES AND APPLICATIONS OF ISLAMIC TREATMENT AND HEALING

1   Introduction 11

2   Islamic Beliefs Related to Causes of Diseases and Their Cures 14

3   Islamic Spiritual Healing Versus Medical Science 17

   3.1   Medical Treatments from an Islamic Standpoint 17

   3.2   Spiritual Treatment and Healing 20

4   Reality of Jinns and Shaytan (Satan) 27

   4.1   Creation of Jinn 28

   4.2   Jinn-Worship by Humans 28

   4.3   Allah Created the Jinn to Worship Him 29

   4.4   Additional Powers of Jinns 32

   4.5   'Iblees' and Shaytan (Satan) – A Creature from the Jinn   32

   4.6   How Jinn and Shaytan Hurt Humans? 39

5   The Reality of Sihr (Black Magic) 47

   5.1   Learning Sihr 49

   5.2   Symptoms of Those Affected by Sihr / Evil Eye 52

6   The Reality of "Evil Eye" 54

7   Conditions for Ruqyah Treatment 60

8   The Forbidden Ways of Treatment and Healing............. 62

  8.1   Treatment Using Sihr (Magic)................................ 62

  8.2   The Use of Amulets, etc.................................... 64

  8.3   Using Strange Methods and Rituals....................... 67

9   The Power and Blessings of the Quran...................... 69

  9.1   The Healing Power of the Quran 71

  9.2   Treating non-Muslims with the Quran...................... 74

10   The Power of Remembrance of Allah 76

11   The Power of Dua 82

PART II – RUQYAH (VERSES AND DUAs) FROM QURAN AND SUNNAH

12   Blessings of Certain Quranic Verses from Hadith 86

  12.1 Blessings of Surah Al-Faatihah............................... 87

  12.2 The Blessings of Surah Al-Baqarah......................... 88

  12.3 Blessings of Aayat al-Kursiy 89

  12.4 The Blessings of Last Verses of Surah Al-Baqarah . 90

  12.5 The Importance of Mu'wadaitain............................ 90

  12.6 The Blessings of Surah Al-Mulk............................ 91

13   Ruqyah from Quran and Hadith Used for Treatment... 92

  13.1 Essential Ruqyah from Quran................................ 92

  13.2 Essential Dua from Hadith 100

  13.3 More Duas for Treatment................................. 109

  13.4 Comprehensive Quranic Ruqyah Treatment......... 119

14   Considerations in Removal of Sihr............................ 122

15   Considerations in Treating Evil Eye 130

16   Jinn Possession Treatment..................................... 134

17   Seeking Protection from Shaytan............................. 136

18   Islamic Guidelines in Treating Physical Ailments 142

19   Ruqyah Guidelines.. 145

20   Other Duas for Well Being 146

    20.1 Dua for Soundness in All Affairs 146

    20.2 Duas for Depression and Anxiety and Psychological
    Problems 148

21   Coping with Life's Trials, Hardships, and Afflictions .. 151

    21.1 The Burdern of Sins... 152

    21.2 Handling of Calamities by the Prophets................. 154

    21.3 Handling Calamities and Challenges in Life 157

22   Appendix I – 37 Verses with "La Ilaha IllAllah".......... 168

23   References... 178

24   Other Books by IqraSense 179

PART I

PRINCIPLES AND APPLICATIONS OF ISLAMIC TREATMENT AND HEALING

1 Introduction

Good health is a blessing that Allah has bestowed upon the children of Adam. However, almost everyone at some time will experience various forms of illness, sometimes minor and occasionally severe. Whatever the cause, medical treatments can provide a cure for many diseases. However, despite advances in treating illness, not all diseases can be accurately diagnosed or treated. A number of them also go untreated because the symptoms of those illnesses are wrongly attributed to other diseases causing people to seek wrong treatments.

Islam has brought to light certain aliments that cannot be characterized by science. These include evil eye, jinn possession, and sihr (witchcraft). Effects of such ailments can cause significant harm, the treatment of which is found in Islamic teachings.

The symptoms of these ailments can be quite similar to those of real physical and psychological diseases, making the diagnosis and treatment quite difficult. Illnesses resulting from the evil eye, sihr (witchcraft), and jinn possession, cannot be treated by advancement in sciences. In such cases, however, religious teachings can provide the needed cure and benefits. But if people do not have that knowledge or do not use them because of their beliefs, the ailment and problems may remain untreated.

Islam does not discourage the use of treatments available through the various sciences. On the contrary, the use of such treatments is encouraged by the teachings of the noble prophet (s.a.w.) who sought the treatment of illnesses and diseases for himself and urged his followers to do the same. Thus, seeking medical treatment for the cure of diseases is part of the prophet's tradition.

We find in a saheeh hadith that the prophet (s.a.w.) said the following:

> *"For every disease there is a medicine, and if that medicine is applied to the disease, he will recover by Allah's Leave." And he (s.a.w.) said: "Allah has not sent down any disease but He has also sent down the cure; the one who knows it, knows it and the one who does not know it, does not know it."*

Based on the above, it is clear that Islamic teachings fully support the use of all forms of treatment because the underlying principle is that Allah has created cures for all diseases. The key is to ensure that the right type of treatment is applied for the right type of ailment. The only condition in Islam is that all forms of treatment are allowed as long as they are not *haram* (against Islamic teachings).

The prophet (s.a.w.) also said,

> *"Allah has sent down the disease and the cure, and has made for every disease the cure. So treat sickness, but do not use anything haram (illegal from an Islamic standpoint)"* (Reported by Abu Dawood, 3376).

As for treatment, Islam offers its believers the opportunity to treat ailments using **ruqyah** that, according to Islamic beliefs, can be used in the treatment of all forms of ailment. *Ruqyah* refers to Quranic verses (and dua) that are used to treat various ailments. The scholars have stated the following about ruqyah:

> *"Ruqyah" is an incantation or prayer for healing – usually from the Quran or dua prescribed by the prophet (s.a.w.). Ruqyah is one of the greatest remedies that the believer should use regularly. The greatest of ruqyah are Surah Al-Faatihah and Al-Mu'wadaitain (the last two surahs (chapters) of the Quran – Surah Al-Falaq and Surah Al-naas) (islamqa.info).*

Islamic beliefs stipulate that each disease is sent down in this world with its cure, but the means of treatment may not be known to everyone. While medical sciences may have helped in the discovery of cures for many diseases and ailments, there are many for which the cures still have to be found. Quranic ruqyah, on the other hand, provides Muslim believers the opportunity to treat all their ailments through the use of Allah's words and duas taught by the prophet (s.a.w.) in parallel with using medical treatments. Ruqyah and other duas taught by the prophet (s.a.w.) can also be used to treat ailments such as sihr, evil eye and jinn possession, which are not recognized and proven by medical sciences.

The duas and ruqyah provided in this book provides us the opportunity to seek protection from all evils by asking Allah's Grace and seeking power through His words to outweigh the evil forces and their harmful effects in our lives.

The chapters in the remainder of this book are divided into two parts. The first part discusses spiritual treatment of ruqyah and treatment using Islamic guidelines versus medical science. The first part also includes chapters that shed light on the reality of Jinn, evil eye, jinn possession and sihr (magic / witchcraft).

The second part of this book includes chapters that list the specific ruqyah available through Quran and hadith of the prophet (s.a.w.) that can be used in the treatment of the various ailments. Almost all of the teachings of this book are based on Islamic guidelines as covered by the Quran, the prophet (s.a.w.) and Islamic scholars' interpretation of those teachings.

The final chapter of this book provides Islamic guidance on dealing with hardships and challenges in life.

2 Islamic Beliefs Related to Causes of Diseases and Their Cures

Before seeking cures for any disease, a Muslim should first believe that all diseases as well as their cures are in Allah's hands and power. Allah alone decrees trials for His creation and He alone can decree their remedies. All means of getting sick and healed are, therefore, contingent upon Allah's decree. As part of a Muslim's belief, this principle is important because people sometimes fail to understand how afflictions come down upon a person and seek their cures without internalizing this reality. So, Allah is the One Who heals whomsoever He wills, and He decrees sickness and death for whomsoever He wills. Some of the Quranic verses related to this are the following:

﴿وَإِن يَمْسَسْكَ اللَّهُ بِضُرٍّ فَلَا كَاشِفَ لَهُ إِلَّا هُوَ ۖ وَإِن يَمْسَسْكَ بِخَيْرٍ فَهُوَ عَلَىٰ كُلِّ شَيْءٍ قَدِيرٌ﴾

"And if Allah touches you with harm, none can remove it but He, and if He touches you with good, then He is Able to do all things" [Surah Al-AnAam, 6:17]

﴿إِنَّمَا أَمْرُهُ إِذَا أَرَادَ شَيْئًا أَن يَقُولَ لَهُ كُن فَيَكُونُ﴾

"Verily, His Command, when He intends a thing, is only that He says to it, 'Be!' and it is! [Surah Yaa-Seen, 36:82]

﴿وَمَا تَشَاءُونَ إِلَّا أَن يَشَاءَ اللَّهُ رَبُّ الْعَالَمِينَ﴾

"And you cannot will unless (it be) that Allah wills the Lord of the Aalameen (mankind, jinn and all that exists) [Surah Al-Takweer, 81:29]

وَإِن يَمْسَسْكَ اللَّهُ بِضُرٍّ فَلَا كَاشِفَ لَهُ إِلَّا هُوَ ۖ وَإِن يُرِدْكَ بِخَيْرٍ فَلَا رَادَّ لِفَضْلِهِ ۚ يُصِيبُ بِهِ مَن يَشَاءُ مِنْ عِبَادِهِ ۚ وَهُوَ الْغَفُورُ الرَّحِيمُ

"And if Allah touches you with harm, there is none who can remove it but He, and if He intends any good for you, there is none who can repel His favor which He causes it to reach whomsoever of His slaves He wills. And He is the Oft-Forgiving, the Most Merciful" [Surah Yunus, 10:107].

The next principle to understand in this context is that any kind of treatment, whether for physical or spiritual illnesses, can never be guaranteed. Allah decides all matters of His entire creation and if a certain kind of treatment is not meant to cure a person then no amount of that treatment can benefit that person. We often observe this in real life, where sometimes even the most skilled physicians and medical professionals fail to treat a person in spite of their great knowledge or experience. Allah says in the Quran:

وَلَن يُؤَخِّرَ اللَّهُ نَفْسًا إِذَا جَاءَ أَجَلُهَا

"And Allah grants respite to none when his appointed time (death) comes" [Surah Al-Munaafiqoon, 63:11].

Shaykh Al-Allaamah Abd Al-Azeez ibn Baaz stated the following:

"Medical treatment is of benefit when the appointed time has not yet come, and Allah decrees that His slave should be

healed. The same applies in the case of one who has been affected by sihr (black magic); Allah may decree that he should recover, or He may not decree that, as a test and a trial, or for other reasons which are known only to Allah. Among those reasons may be the fact that the one who is treating him does not have the right treatment for this problem. It was narrated in a saheeh report that the prophet (s.a.w.) said: "For every disease there is a medicine, and if that medicine is applied to the disease, he will recover by Allah's Leave." And he (s.a.w.) said: "Allah has not sent down any disease but He has also sent down the cure; the one who knows it knows it and the one who does not know it does not know it."

[Source: Majmoo' Fataawa wa Maqaalaat Mutanawwiah li Samaahat Al-Shaykh Al-Allaamah Abd Al-Azeez ibn Baaz (may Allah have mercy on him), p. 70]

3 Islamic Spiritual Healing Versus Medical Science

As Muslims, we are fortunate to have available to us the means of both physical and spiritual treatments for the cure of our diseases. However, some people exclusively rely on medical (physical) treatment whereas there are some who only use the spiritual cures and medicines that are known through the Quran and hadith. This chapter sheds light on both schools of thought and highlights the Islamic viewpoint through the Quran and hadith, and the views of renowned scholars.

3.1 Medical Treatments from an Islamic Standpoint

As Allah – the Creator – has created the diseases, He has also created their cures that exist in the physical world. We noted this in a hadith mentioned earlier in which the prophet (s.a.w.) had mentioned that Allah has not sent down any disease without sending down its cure as well. Most Islamic scholars, therefore, agree that seeking cure from medical sciences is perfectly valid because all kinds of cures, whether known through the medical sciences or spiritual means, are from Allah. The only condition for such treatments is that they should not specifically violate Islamic guidelines. A person, therefore, can use both forms of treatments (medical and spiritual) to treat one's illnesses and ailments.

According to a hadith of the prophet (s.a.w.):

> *Abu'l-Darda' (may Allah be pleased with him) reported that: "The Messenger of Allah (s.a.w.) said: Allah has sent down the disease and the cure, and has made for every disease*

the cure. So treat sickness, but do not use anything haram (illegal)" (Reported by Abu Dawood, 3376).

Usaamah ibn Shurayk (may Allah be pleased with him) reported: 'The Bedouin said, "O Messenger of Allah, should we not treat sickness?" He said: "Treat sickness, for Allah has not created any disease except He has also created the cure, except for one disease." They said, "O Messenger of Allah, what is it?" He said: "Old age."' (Reported by Al-Tirmidhi, 4/383, no. 1961. He said: This is a saheeh hasan hadeeth. See also Saheeh Al-Jaami', 2930.)

Consider the following that is stated in Fateh al Haq:

"There are beneficial natural medicines, which are supported by the Quran and Sunnah. If they are taken by a person with faith and belief that the benefit comes only from Allah, then Allah will In Sha Allah benefit him. There are also other medicines which are made using substances such as plant extracts and other sources and their benefits are established based on experimentations and observations. There is nothing wrong in the use of those medicines from an Islamic viewpoint as long as they (or substances used in them) are not specifically known to be haram." [Source: Fatah al Haq al Mubeen fee Eelaaj al-Saraa' wa al-sahar wa al-a'in, Page 139).]

One may ask whether the use of spiritual treatments based on the Quran and sunnah is in contradiction to those based on medical sciences. We know from the prophet's life that he (s.a.w.) used the Quran and dua to treat all types of ailments along with using physical means of healing. The use of medical treatment, therefore, does not contradict any Islamic guidelines nor should it suppress one's belief and trust (tawakkul) in Allah. The proper way, therefore, is to fully trust Allah, to ask for His help, and to seek medical advice as well. In this context, Ibn Al-Qayyim stated the following:

"This (seeking medical advice) does not contradict tawaakul (putting one's trust in Allah), just as warding off hunger, thirst, heat and cold does not contradict tawakkul. The essence of tawaakul is not complete without resorting to the means which Allah has set out in order for us to achieve results both according to His decree (qadr) and His laws. Not using these means is contrary to tawakkul: it goes against and undermines the command and wisdom of Allah, although the one who neglects the means may think that this makes his tawakkul stronger. Ignoring the means is a sign of helplessness that goes against the true essence of tawakkul, which is that the heart relies on Allah to bring the slave whatever will benefit him in this world and the next, and to protect him from whatever may harm him in this world and the next. But along with this reliance, it is essential to take the appropriate means, otherwise he will be going against the wisdom and command of Allah. Helplessness should not be taken as a sign of tawaakul, nor should tawakkul make a person helpless (Zaad Al-MaAad, 4/15. See Al-MawsooAh Al-Fiqhiyyah, 11/116).

Those who may have doubts about using non-spiritual mechanisms to treat ailments and diseases should note that the prophet (s.a.w.) used cupping and other physical remedies to treat certain ailments. This, therefore, according to most scholars, clearly lends credibility to the use of non-spiritual forms of treatment. Although there may be some difference of opinions within the *Ahlus-sunnah* (followers of the prophet's traditions), yet no one disallows the use of medical treatment, particularly when no other means are available. For example, according to the majority of Hanafi and Maaliki school of thought, medical treatment is mubaah (permitted), whereas the Shaafi'is, and Al-Qaadi, Ibn Aqeel and Ibn Al-Jawzi among the Hanbalis, say that it is *mustahabb* (recommended). This is based on the hadith mentioned earlier that stated, *"Allah has sent down the disease and the cure, and has made for every disease the cure. So treat sickness, but do not use anything haram..."* [(Haashiyat Ibn

Aabideen, 5/215, 249; Al-Hidaayah Takmilat Fath Al-Qadeer, 8/134; Al-Aadaab Al-Shar'iyyah, 2/359ff, Haashiyat Al-Jumal, 2/134).

3.2 Spiritual Treatment and Healing

Spiritual treatment in Islam or *ruqyah* refers to the use of Allah's words that He revealed in the Quran and what He taught the prophet (s.a.w.) to treat various ailments. The Quran is the word of the Superme Being – Allah – who created everything. The Creator has clearly told us that the words of the Quran are "shifa" (healing) for all and, therefore, when used with real belief in one's heart, this form of treatment can bring miraculous cure to all forms of ailments.

Allah says in the Quran:

﴿وَنُنَزِّلُ مِنَ الْقُرْآنِ مَا هُوَ شِفَاءٌ وَرَحْمَةٌ لِّلْمُؤْمِنِينَ﴾

"And We send down of the Quran that which is a healing and a mercy to those who believe..." (Quran, Surah Al-Israa, 17:82).

﴿وَإِذَا مَرِضْتُ فَهُوَ يَشْفِينِ﴾

And when I am ill, it is [God] who cures me" (Surah ash-Shu`ara, 26:80) (A supplication of Prophet Abraham [a.s.]).

While physical ailments can be treated through the application of medical science, the problems related to evil eye, sihr (witchcraft), jinn possession, and any conditions or ailments that are brought upon by *Shayateen* (devils – plural for Shaytaan or Satan) can only be treated through Quranic ruqyah. This is because these ailments are non-physical, and as they cannot be proven scientifically, medical science has no cures for them. This is the reason why the Quran and dua from hadith are used as the primary methods for the treatment of such ailments.

Treatment through ruqyah from the Quran and Hadith is beneficial only when one has complete faith in Allah and His power to treat the disease. As mentioned earlier, we should remind ourselves that as Muslims, we believe that all matters rest in the hands of Allah alone and nothing can happen without His will. A person, therefore, cannot get sick without Allah's permission and similarly cannot get cured without His permission. When curing any person with the verses of the Quran and when making Dua to Allah, one of the foremost conditions to expect any cure is to believe in the power of the words of Allah and to also believe in the fact that He alone can cure all types of ailments. The treatment is even more effective when both the reciter of the Quranic verses and the patient have complete faith in Allah's words and they trust only in Allah's will to treat the ailment of the patient. The book Jawab-il-Kafi states the following:

وَكَذَلِكَ الْعِلاَجُ بِالرُّقَى النَّبَوِيَّةِ الثَّابِتَةِ مِنْ أَنْفَعِ الأَدْوِيَةِ،

وَالدُّعَاءُ إِذَا سَلِمَ مِنَ الْمَوَانِعِ مِنْ أَنْفَعِ الأَسْبَابِ فِي دَفْعِ

الْمَكْرُوهِ، وَحُصُولِالْمَطْلُوبِ، فَهُوَ مِنْ أَنْفَعِ الأَدْوِيَةِ، وَخَاصَّةً

مَعَ الإِلْحَاحِ فِيهِ، وَهُوَ عَدُوُّ الْبَلاَءِ، يُدَافِعُهُ وَيُعَالِجُهُ، وَيَمْنَعُ

نُزُولَهُ، أَوْ يُخَفِّفُهُ إِذَا نَزَلَ

And the cure using Ruqyah of the prophet (s.a.w.) is proven to be the most beneficial of the medicines. And, if the dua does not include any prohibited aspects, it is the most beneficial means of ridding one of any undesired effects, and to ask for what one wants. Thus, it is one of the most important medicines, especially when one makes a dua by pleading to Allah as it can repel challenges, and protects one from them and can even cure one from it or diminish their effect if one faces them.

[Source: Al-Jawab-il-Kaafi, Pages 22 – 25]

Ibn Hajar mentioned the following:

الرُّقَى بِالْمُعَوِّذَتِ وَغَيْرِهَا مِنْ أَسْمَاءِ اللَّهِ هُوَ الطِّبُّ الرُّوحَانِيُّ إِذَا كَانَ عَلَى لِسَانِ الْأَبْرَارِ مِنَ الْخَلْقِ حَصَلَ الشِّفَاءُ بِإِذْنِ اللَّهِ تَعَالَى

"Ruqyah by recitation of Muawwidat (last two surahs of Quran) or other Quranic verses using names of Allah is spiritual medicine. If it is performed at the tongues of the righteous and pious, it can result in healing with the will of Allah." [Source: Fathal-Bari (196/10).]

Those who doubt the reality of cures that cannot be proven through medical science should know that not all knowledge of this life and universe can be known through the use of observation and reason alone. Allah's creation, as well as the knowledge of that creation, transcends our observations and everything else that can be proven through physical means. Although Allah has provided us some knowledge of what we observe in the physical world and about the unseen through His prophets and their revelations, yet a vast amount of the knowledge is not made known to us. As an example of this, consider the following verse that Allah mentions in the Quran:

﴿وَيَسْأَلُونَكَ عَنِ الرُّوحِ ۖ قُلِ الرُّوحُ مِنْ أَمْرِ رَبِّي وَمَا أُوتِيتُم مِّنَ الْعِلْمِ إِلَّا قَلِيلًا﴾

'Say (O Muhammad (s.a.w.)): "The Rooh (the Spirit): it is one of the things, the knowledge of which is only with

my Lord. And of knowledge, you (mankind) have been given only a little"' (Surah Al-Isra, 17:85).

Thus, we know from religious teachings that while we can rely on observation and reason for the discovery of most of what we know in this life, yet there are other facts that we have come to know only through religious and divine teachings. The following is an excerpt from the writings of Ibn Taymiyyah on this topic that shows that complete knowledge (as much as Allah wants us to know) requires dependence on both: reason as well as prophetic revelations.

Reason is a prerequisite to the acquisition of knowledge, as well as for the performance of a good deed or righteous act. Mystical states like ecstasy or intoxication, which involve the suppression of reason, are imperfect states of mind, and ideas that conflict with reason are false. However, reason is not self-sufficient; it cannot dispense with revelation, which alone gives the knowledge of realities that transcend it.

Many theologians base their ideas simply on reason, and rely exclusively on it. They subject it to the faith and the Quran. Knowledge is derived from general principles of reason sufficient in themselves without recourse to faith in the Quran.

... To be sure, reason is prerequisite to all knowledge, as it is the prerequisite of virtue and good life. With it we acquire knowledge and virtue, but it is not sufficient by itself. It is only a faculty of the soul, a power like the power of vision in the eye. It works only when it receives light from faith and the Quran, as the eye sees only when it receives light from the sun or a fire.

Left to itself, reason cannot know things which it is not equipped to know by itself. On the other hand, when it is completely suppressed, the ideas that one receives and the acts that one performs may be things such as happen to the animals. One may have love and ecstasy and other experiences, but they will not be different from what the animals get. Hence the states that one attains by negating reason are defective, and the ideas one receives contrary to reason are false.

Prophets came with knowledge which reason could not attain in and of itself; never did they come with what reason considers to be impossible. People who place unjustified faith in reason readily make statements regarding the necessity, possibility or impossibility of things purely on the basis of reason; they work all the while under the impression that their views are correct, whereas they are false; they are even audacious enough to oppose the views which the prophets taught. On the other hand, those who decry reason and affirm things that are false, revel in satanic states and evil practices, and cross the boundaries which the sense of discrimination (between good and evil) draws, with which God has endowed man and elevated him above other creatures.

Among the people of hadith (ahl al-hadith) there are also some who lean towards one or the other of these two groups. They sometimes bring down reason from its position, and sometimes put it against the prophetic practices (sunan). [Source: Ibn Taymiyyah Fatawa 3:338-9 – Taken from "Ibn Taymiyyah Expounds on Islam]

So, one can see that knowledge of complete *shifa* does not lie in just knowing and applying the medical sciences but also in relying on the spiritual treatments that we have learned through prophetic revelations. Furthermore, we also know that cures for different ailments known through medical sciences are being discovered gradually and a vast amount of knowledge yet remains unknown. However, what Allah wishes man to know about spiritual healing has all been revealed to the prophet (s.a.w.) and that he has taught us in turn through the Quran and his sayings. Allah says in the Quran:

الْيَوْمَ أَكْمَلْتُ لَكُمْ دِينَكُمْ وَأَتْمَمْتُ عَلَيْكُمْ نِعْمَتِي
وَرَضِيتُ لَكُمُ الْإِسْلَامَ دِينًا ۞

*"This day have I perfected your religion for you,
completed My favor upon you, and have chosen for
you Islam as your religion" (Surah Al-Ma'idah, 5:3).*

So, the question that one may ask will be whether to seek both
forms of treatment. The answer to this question is that since a
Muslim strongly believes that everything happens by the will of Allah
and only He controls all matters of this world and the hereafter, all
known modes of treatment should be applied in order to cure a
disease, as each mode of treatment is also in the hands of Allah,
the Merciful. On this, Shaykh Ibn Uthaymeen stated:

*Note that medical treatment is a means of healing but the
One Who causes it to be effective is Allah, may He be
exalted. There is no cause except that which Allah makes a
cause. The things that Allah makes causes are of two types:*

*Means that are prescribed in shareeah, such as the Holy
Quran and dua (supplication), as the prophet (s.a.w.) said
concerning Surah Al-Faatihah: "How did you know that it is a
ruqyah (prayer or incantation for healing)?" And the prophet
(s.a.w.) recited ruqyah for the sick by making dua for them,
and Allah healed those whom He wanted to heal by virtue of
his dua.*

*Physical means may be medicines that are known from
shareeah like honey, or from experimentation and
experience, like many kinds of medicine. The effect of this
kind of means must be direct, not by way of imagination and
wishful thinking. If its effect is known in a direct and
measurable manner, then it may rightfully be used as a
remedy by means of which a cure may be effected, by*

Allah's leave. But if it is simply the matter of wishful thinking on the part of the patient, which brings him some kind of psychological relief, then it is not permissible to rely on it or affirm that it is a remedy, lest a person come to depend on wishful thinking. Hence it is forbidden to wear rings, strings, etc., to heal disease or ward it off, because that is not a means that is prescribed in shareeah or known from experience. So long as it is not proven to be a means that is prescribed in shareeah or known from experience, it is not permissible to regard it as a means of healing. Regarding it as a means is a kind of trying to compete with Allah in His dominion and associating others with Him, in the sense that one is trying to play a role that belongs only to Allah, namely deciding the means and the ends. Shaykh Muhammad ibn Abd Al-Wahhaab explained this matter in Kitaab Al-Tawheed by saying: "It is shirk (associating others with Allah or with His powers) to wear rings and strings, etc., to ward off evil or relieve it." [Source: Majmoo' Fataawa Al-Shaykh Ibn Uthaymeen, 1, question no. 49.]

4 Reality of Jinns and Shaytan (Satan)

Jinns or spirits, like everything else, are a creation of Allah. The Quran has numerous references about their existence. The Jinns are part of the unseen world and their existence, therefore, cannot be proven through any of the physical sciences. Reported sightings of Jinns or ghosts, along with experiences of the unseen, however, are too frequent for anyone to discount. Although such activity is not clearly defined and proven by the physical sciences, yet very few deny the existence of these unseen creatures.

Jinns are one of the many creatures of Allah and belief in their existence is part of Islamic faith. This is because they are mentioned in the Quran and there are numerous hadith about them. Ibn Hazm said: *"The jinn are real, and they are creatures created by Allah. Among them are kaafirs and believers. They can see us but we cannot see them. They eat, have children and die" (al-Muhallaa, 1/34/35).* In Judeo-Christian religions, although the word "Jinn" is not mentioned, references to 'ghosts' can be found both in the Torah and the Bible. Besides, the Arabic word of "Jinn" can be found in old Arabic translations of the Bible. Other religions, too, have various forms of references and beliefs related to jinn and / or ghosts.

Shaykh al-Islam Ibn Taymiyah said: *"All nations believe in the jinn and they have had many encounters with them, which it would take too long to describe. No one denies the existence of the jinn except for a very few ignorant philosophers and doctors and the like."* [Source: Majmoo' al-Fataawa, 19/32]

The following sections shed more light on the reality of Jinns from an Islamic standpoint.

4.1 Creation of Jinn

Allah has created Adam and mankind from mud (earth) while He created jinn from fire and the angels from light. Allah says in the Quran:

$$﴿وَخَلَقَ الْجَانَّ مِن مَّارِجٍ مِّن نَّارٍ﴾$$

"And the jinn He created from a smokeless flame of fire" [Surah al-Rahmaan, 55:15].

And He describes in the Holy Quaran how Iblees addressed the Lord of Glory (may He be glorified and exalted):

$$﴿قَالَ أَنَا خَيْرٌ مِّنْهُ خَلَقْتَنِي مِن نَّارٍ وَخَلَقْتَهُ مِن طِينٍ﴾$$

"I am better than him (Adam), You created me from fire, and him You created from clay" [Surah al-A'raaf, 7:12].

Allah says in the Quran:

$$﴿وَلَقَدْ خَلَقْنَا الْإِنسَانَ مِن صَلْصَالٍ مِّنْ حَمَإٍ مَّسْنُونٍ﴾$$

$$﴿وَالْجَانَّ خَلَقْنَاهُ مِن قَبْلُ مِن نَّارِ السَّمُومِ﴾$$

"And indeed, We created man from dried (sounding) clay of altered mud.
And the jinn, We created aforetime from the smokeless flame of fire" [Sura al-Hijr, 15:26-27].

4.2 Jinn-Worship by Humans

'Devil worship' is found in many parts of the world. Such worship predates the time before Islam. For example, inscriptions found in Northwest Arabia from the pre-Islamic era seem to indicate Jinn-worship. For instance, an inscription from Beth Fasi'el near Palmyra (ancient city in Syria) pays tribute to the "Jinnaye", who were considered gods at that time [Source: Arabia and the Arabs: from the Bronze Age to the coming of Islam, By Robert Hoyland].

The Quran, too, mentions the practice of jinn worship in the following verse:

وَجَعَلُوا لِلَّهِ شُرَكَاءَ الْجِنَّ وَخَلَقَهُمْ ۖ وَخَرَقُوا لَهُ بَنِينَ وَبَنَاتٍ بِغَيْرِ عِلْمٍ ۚ سُبْحَانَهُ وَتَعَالَىٰ عَمَّا يَصِفُونَ

"Yet, they join the jinn as partners in worship with Allah, though He has created them (the jinn), and they attribute falsely without knowledge sons and daughters to Him. Be He glorified and exalted above (all) that they attribute to Him" (Surah Al-Anaam, 6:100).

4.3 Allah Created the Jinn to Worship Him

Allah created the jinn and mankind to worship Him. The following verses in the Quran attest to that fact.

وَمَا خَلَقْتُ الْجِنَّ وَالْإِنسَ إِلَّا لِيَعْبُدُونِ

مَا أُرِيدُ مِنْهُم مِّن رِّزْقٍ وَمَا أُرِيدُ أَن يُطْعِمُونِ

إِنَّ اللَّهَ هُوَ الرَّزَّاقُ ذُو الْقُوَّةِ الْمَتِينُ

- *"And I (Allah) created not the jinn and mankind except that they should worship Me (alone).*
- *I seek not any provision from them (i.e. provision for themselves or for My creatures) nor do I ask that they should feed Me (i.e. feed themselves or My creatures).*

- **Verily, Allah is the All Provider, Owner of Power, the Most Strong" [Surah al-Dhaariyaat, 51:56]**

Jinn, like mankind, therefore, are accountable for their actions and thus will be punished and rewarded according to their deeds. The following Quranic verses provide us with proof. Allah says in the Quran:

The jinn say (as stated in the Quran):

﴿وَأَنَّا مِنَّا الصَّالِحُونَ وَمِنَّا دُونَ ذَلِكَ ۖ كُنَّا طَرَائِقَ قِدَدًا﴾

"'There are among us some that are righteous, and some the contrary; we are groups having different ways (religious sects)'" [Surah al-Jinn, 72:11].

﴿وَأَنَّا مِنَّا الْمُسْلِمُونَ وَمِنَّا الْقَاسِطُونَ ۖ فَمَنْ أَسْلَمَ فَأُولَئِكَ تَحَرَّوْا رَشَدًا﴾

"And of us some are Muslims (who have submitted to Allah, after listening to this Quran), and of us some are Al-Qaasitoon (disbelievers, those who have deviated from the Right Path)'. And whosoever has embraced Islam (i.e. has become a Muslim by submitting to Allah), then such have sought the Right Path.'

﴿وَأَمَّا الْقَاسِطُونَ فَكَانُوا لِجَهَنَّمَ حَطَبًا﴾

And as for the Qaasitoon (disbelievers who deviated from the Right Path), they shall be firewood for Hell" [Surah al-Jinn, 72:14-15].

Once when the Messenger (s.a.w.) was in Makkah, a group of Jinns appeared to him upon hearing the recitation of the holy Quran. They were moved to such an extent that they said the following (as mentioned in the Quran):

$$﴿وَإِذْ صَرَفْنَا إِلَيْكَ نَفَرًا مِّنَ الْجِنِّ يَسْتَمِعُونَ الْقُرْآنَ فَلَمَّا حَضَرُوهُ قَالُوا أَنصِتُوا ۖ فَلَمَّا قُضِيَ وَلَّوْا إِلَىٰ قَوْمِهِم مُّنذِرِينَ﴾$$

"And (remember) when We sent towards you (Muhammad) a group (three to ten persons) of the jinn, (quietly) listening to the Quran. When they stood in the presence thereof, they said: "Listen in silence!" And when it was finished, they returned to their people, as warners" [Surah al-Ahqaaf, 46:29].

The Quran tells us that upon hearing the Quran, some of the jinn believed in Allah and His message to the prophet (s.a.w.). Allah says:

$$﴿قُلْ أُوحِيَ إِلَيَّ أَنَّهُ اسْتَمَعَ نَفَرٌ مِّنَ الْجِنِّ فَقَالُوا إِنَّا سَمِعْنَا قُرْآنًا عَجَبًا﴾$$

"Say (O Muhammad): 'It has been revealed to me that a group (from three to ten in number) of jinn listened (to this Quran). They said: "Verily, we have heard a wonderful Recitation (this Quran)!

$$﴿يَهْدِي إِلَى الرُّشْدِ فَآمَنَّا بِهِ ۖ وَلَن نُّشْرِكَ بِرَبِّنَا أَحَدًا﴾$$

It guides to the Right Path, and we have believed therein, and we shall never join (in worship) anything with our Lord (Allah) [Surah al-Jinn, 72:1-2].

4.4 Additional Powers of Jinns

Allah has created jinns with different powers. Consider the following verse:

﴿قَالَ عِفْرِيتٌ مِّنَ الْجِنِّ أَنَا آتِيكَ بِهِ قَبْلَ أَن تَقُومَ مِن مَّقَامِكَ﴾

"An Ifreet (strong one) from the jinn said (to Prophet Sulaiman): "I will bring it [the throne of the Queen of Saba] to you before you rise from your place" [Surah al-Naml, 27:39].

Also, though the jinns co-exist with us on this earth, they see us but we do not see them, as Allah says of Iblees and his tribe:

﴿إِنَّهُ يَرَاكُمْ هُوَ وَقَبِيلُهُ مِنْ حَيْثُ لَا تَرَوْنَهُمْ﴾

"Verily, he and Qabeeluhu (his soldiers from the jinn or his tribe) see you from where you cannot see them" [Surah al-A'raaf, 7:27].

4.5 'Iblees' and Shaytan (Satan) – A Creature from the Jinn

As mentioned in the earlier section, the Shaytan is from the evil / Kuffars of the jinn and is one of the worst enemies of mankind and is known through the Quran and hadith to inflict the most harm on humans. Knowing about Shayateen (devils – plural of Shaytan) and their tactics in hurting people, therefore, is important. Allah sent the prophets to guide humanity and therefore, shayateen resisted their efforts by trying to hurt them the most. Allah says in the Quran:

﴾وَكَذَلِكَ جَعَلْنَا لِكُلِّ نَبِيٍّ عَدُوًّا شَيَاطِينَ الْإِنسِ وَالْجِنِّ يُوحِي بَعْضُهُمْ إِلَىٰ بَعْضٍ زُخْرُفَ الْقَوْلِ غُرُورًا﴾

(And so We have appointed for every Prophet enemies – Shayateen among mankind and jinn – inspiring one another with adorned speech as a delusion.) (Surah Al-Anaam, 6:112)

Iblees, who is mentioned a number of times in the Quran, is also a creature from among the jinn. Allah says in the Quran:

﴾إِلَّا إِبْلِيسَ كَانَ مِنَ الْجِنِّ فَفَسَقَ عَنْ أَمْرِ رَبِّهِ﴾

"except Iblees (Satan). He was one of the jinn; he disobeyed the Command of his Lord" [Surah al-Kahf, 18:50].

So, it is clear that all shayateen (devils) are the kuffar of the jinn because there are many amongst the jinn who are righteous as well. As for the relationship of Iblees to the jinn, the popular view amongst the scholars is that Iblees is the father of the jinn just the same way as Prophet Adam is the father of humans [Tafseer al-Tabari (1/507) and al-Durr al-Manthoor (5/402)]. Just as Adam had descendents, so Iblees had descendents too, as Allah says of Iblees:

﴾أَفَتَتَّخِذُونَهُ وَذُرِّيَّتَهُ أَوْلِيَاءَ مِن دُونِي وَهُمْ لَكُمْ عَدُوٌّ بِئْسَ لِلظَّالِمِينَ بَدَلًا﴾

"Will you then take him (Iblees) and his offspring as protectors and helpers rather than Me while they are

enemies to you? What an evil is the exchange for the Zaalimoon (wrongdoers, etc)" [Surah al-Kahf, 18:50].

Shaykh al-Islam Ibn Taymiyah also called Iblees the father of the jinn in more than one place (Majmoo' al-Fataawa, 4/346, 235), as did his student Ibn al-Qayyim, then al-Haafiz Ibn Hajar in Fath al-Baari (6/369). Shaykh Abd al-Azeez ibn Baaz said in Majmoo' al-Fataawa (9/370-371) the following: *"The Shaytan is the father of the jinn according to a number of scholars. He is the one who disobeyed his Lord and was too proud to prostrate to Adam, so Allah expelled him and cast him away."*

Ibn Katheer said in his Tafseer: *"Al-Hasan al-Basri said: Iblees was not one of the angels, not even for a single moment. He is the father of the jinn, just as Adam (peace be upon him) is the father of mankind" [Narrated by al-Tabari with a saheeh isnaad (part 3/89)].*

Shaykh Ibn Uthaymeen stated: *"This evidence clearly indicates that Iblees has offspring and that the jinn are his offspring, but how did that come about? This is something of which we have no knowledge and it is something concerning which it does not matter if we are ignorant, and knowing it does not bring any benefit. And Allah knows best [al-Jinn wa'l-Shayaateen, question no. 2, Fataawa Noor Ala al-Darb]."*

Many Islamic texts have provided explanations about Iblees, Shayateen, and Jinn. However, one should be careful in believing in those reports as some of them come from other religions but are not proven by Islam. Ibn Katheer said, explaining this:

> *"A lot of reports (about Shaytan and Jinn) were transmitted from the Salaf (followers of the prophet and his ways), and most of them come from the Israa'eeliyyaat, which may have been transmitted in order to be examined [i.e., as opposed to being accepted as is]. Allah knows best about the veracity of many of them. Some of them are definitely to be rejected, because they go against the truth which we hold in our hands. In the Quran we have sufficient (proofs) so that we have no need of previous reports, because hardly any of*

them are free of distortions, with things added or taken away. Many things have been fabricated in them, for they did not have people who had memorized things precisely by heart (huffaaz) who could eliminate the distortions created by extremists and fabricators, unlike this ummah which has its imaams, scholars, masters, pious and righteous people, brilliant critics and men of excellent memory who recorded the hadeeths and classified them, stating whether they were saheeh (sound), hasan (good), da'eef (weak), mawdoo' (fabricated), matrook (to be ignored). They identified the fabricators and liars, and those about whom nothing was known, and other kinds of men (i.e., narrators). All of this afforded protection to the prophet (s.a.w.), the Seal of the Messengers and the Leader of Mankind, so that nothing would be attributed to him falsely and nothing would be transmitted from him that he did not say or do. (Tafseer al-Quran il-Azeem, 3/90)."

The difference between Iblees and Adam was that although both transgressed Allah's commands, Adam repented to Allah later and was forgiven. However, Iblees was too proud to repent.

Allah says in the Quran:

$$\text{﴿فَتَلَقَّىٰ آدَمُ مِن رَّبِّهِ كَلِمَاتٍ فَتَابَ عَلَيْهِ ۚ إِنَّهُ هُوَ التَّوَّابُ الرَّحِيمُ﴾}$$

"Then Adam received from his Lord Words. And his Lord pardoned him (accepted his repentance). Verily, He is the One Who forgives (accepts repentance), the Most Merciful" [Surah al-Baqarah, 2:37].

As for Iblees, Allah says in the Quran:

﴿وَإِذْ قُلْنَا لِلْمَلَائِكَةِ اسْجُدُوا لِآدَمَ فَسَجَدُوا إِلَّا إِبْلِيسَ أَبَىٰ
وَاسْتَكْبَرَ وَكَانَ مِنَ الْكَافِرِينَ﴾

"And (remember) when We said to the angels: 'Prostrate yourselves before Adam.' And they prostrated except Iblees (Satan), he refused and was proud and was one of the disbelievers (disobedient to Allah)" [Surah al-Baqarah, 2:34].

Allah then said to Iblees:

﴿قَالَ فَالْحَقُّ وَالْحَقَّ أَقُولُ﴾

"(Allah) said: 'The truth is — and the truth I say

لَأَمْلَأَنَّ جَهَنَّمَ مِنكَ وَمِمَّن تَبِعَكَ مِنْهُمْ أَجْمَعِينَ﴾

That I will fill Hell with you [Iblees (Satan)] and those of them (mankind) that follow you, together'" [Surah Saad, 38:84-85].

Allah also tells us in the Quran that the shayateen (devils) and jinn cooperate with each other as mentioned in the verses below:

﴿وَكَذَٰلِكَ جَعَلْنَا لِكُلِّ نَبِيٍّ عَدُوًّا شَيَاطِينَ الْإِنسِ وَالْجِنِّ
يُوحِي بَعْضُهُمْ إِلَىٰ بَعْضٍ زُخْرُفَ الْقَوْلِ غُرُورًا ۚ وَلَوْ شَاءَ
رَبُّكَ مَا فَعَلُوهُ ۖ فَذَرْهُمْ وَمَا يَفْتَرُونَ﴾

"And so We have appointed for every prophet enemies — Shayaateen (devils) among mankind and Jinn, inspiring one another with adorned speech as a

delusion (or by way of deception). If your Lord had so willed, they would not have done it; so leave them alone with their fabrications" [Surah al-AnAam, 6:112].

The jinn used to eavesdrop on the inhabitants of the heavens but later were stopped from doing so, as Allah tells us in the Quran on what the jinns say:

وَأَنَّا لَمَسْنَا السَّمَاءَ فَوَجَدْنَاهَا مُلِئَتْ حَرَسًا شَدِيدًا وَشُهُبًا

"And we (Jinns) have sought to reach the heaven; but found it filled with stern guards and flaming fires.

وَأَنَّا كُنَّا نَقْعُدُ مِنْهَا مَقَاعِدَ لِلسَّمْعِ ۖ فَمَن يَسْتَمِعِ الْآنَ يَجِدْ لَهُ شِهَابًا رَّصَدًا

And verily, we (Jinns) used to sit there in stations, to (steal) a hearing, but any who listens now will find a flaming fire watching him in ambush [Surah al-Jinn, 72:8-9].

We all know about the role of Shaytan in whispering to mankind to do evil acts. In the Quran, Allah refers to this Shaytan as "qareen". A qareen accompanies every human being and it pushes us to do evil deeds.

Allah says:

قَالَ قَرِينُهُ رَبَّنَا مَا أَطْغَيْتُهُ وَلَكِن كَانَ فِي ضَلَالٍ بَعِيدٍ

His companion (qareen) will say: 'Our Lord! I did not push him to transgression, (in disbelief, oppression, and evil deeds), but he was himself in error far astray.'

﴿قَالَ لَا تَخْتَصِمُوا لَدَيَّ وَقَدْ قَدَّمْتُ إِلَيْكُم بِالْوَعِيدِ﴾

Allah will say: 'Dispute not in front of Me, I had already in advance sent you the threat.'

﴿مَا يُبَدَّلُ الْقَوْلُ لَدَيَّ وَمَا أَنَا بِظَلَّامٍ لِّلْعَبِيدِ﴾

The sentence that comes from Me cannot be changed, and I am not unjust to the slaves [Surah Qaaf, 50:27-29].

According to a hadith, the Messenger of Allah (s.a.w.) said:

"… There is assigned to him a companion (qareen) from among the jinn and a companion from among the angels" [Narrated by Muslim, 2814].

Another explanation was given by Al-Shawkaani who said: *"The phrase 'for there is a qareen with him'—according to al-Qaamoos [an Arabic-language dictionary] the word qareen refers to a companion; the Shaytan always accompanies man and never leaves him. This is what is referred to here"* [Nayl al-Awtaar, 3/7].

It is mentioned in Tafsir Ibn Kathir that according to a Saheeh hadith (the prophet said),

«مَا مِنْكُمْ مِنْ أَحَدٍ إِلَّا قَدْ وُكِّلَ بِهِ قَرِينُهُ»

There is not a single one of you except that his companion (a devil) has been assigned to him. They (the Companions) said, "What about you, O Messenger of Allah?" He replied,

«نَعَمْ، إِلَّا أَنَّ اللهَ أَعَانَنِي عَلَيْهِ فَأَسْلَمَ، فَلَا يَأْمُرُنِي إِلَّا بِخَيْرٍ»

Yes. However, Allah has helped me against him and he has accepted Islam. Thus, he only commands me to do good.

As the Qareen always accompanies every person, therefore the prophet (s.a.w.) instructed us not to allow a person to walk in front of a person who is offering his prayers. AbdAllah ibn 'Umar narrated that the Messenger of Allah (s.a.w.) said:

"If anyone of you is praying, he should not let anyone pass in front of him; if that person insists then he should fight him for there is a qareen with him." [Narrated by Muslim, 506]

So, while praying in front of Allah, the qareen should not be allowed to come in between a person's prayers and Allah.

4.6 How Jinn and Shaytan Hurt Humans?

One of the most common ways that jinn can hurt humans is through possession of their bodies. Many people in this life relate such experiences that may be attributed to jinn possession. While it is true that some of these experiences may be psychological in nature and part of a person's illusions, some cases do exist that are actually related to jinn possession.

The treatment and remedy of such experiences, therefore, has to be done carefully by seeking both medical and spiritual advice. Some scholars have commented that *"there are some facts and some illusions connected to the issue of jinn possession, and among most people nowadays the illusions outweigh the facts. The Sunnis are unanimously agreed that the jinn can dwell in the bodies of humans, but that does not mean that everyone who has epilepsy is possessed by the jinn, because epilepsy may have physical causes. The pains that many people feel in their bodies cannot be ascribed for certain to the actions of the jinn, rather they may be illusions or something imaginary." (Source: islamqa.info)*

The Quran clearly refers to the fact of jinn possession. Believing that jinn can possess human beings is, therefore, part of Islamic faith. The word that is used in the Quran in this context is "*Muss*" as it appears in verse 275 of Surah Al-Baqarah. Scholars attribute the following Quranic verse about jinn possession. Allah says in His Book:

$$\text{﴿الَّذِينَ يَأْكُلُونَ الرِّبَا لَا يَقُومُونَ إِلَّا كَمَا يَقُومُ الَّذِي يَتَخَبَّطُهُ الشَّيْطَانُ مِنَ الْمَسِّ﴾}$$

"Those who eat Ribaa [usury / interest] will not stand (on the Day of Resurrection) except like the standing of a person beaten by Shaytan (Satan) leading him to insanity" [Surah al-Baqarah, 2:275].

Allah uses this verse to inform us about the state of a person, in the hereafter, who has taken Ribaa (interest) in this world. Those people will be in such a bad state that they would act in an insane manner. Allah compares their state on the Day of Judgement to that of the one who is possessed by jinn in this world. Scholars who treat jinn possession explain such experiences through visual observation.

Al-Saheeh reports this as narrated by the prophet (s.a.w.):

"The Shaytan flows through the son of Adam like blood." Majmoo' al-Fataawa (24/276, 277)

Jinn's possession can take many forms. A jinn can posses a person's entire body, or parts of the body, or his tongue only. Also, jinn can stay in a person's body for a long duration or for only a few moments in a person's dream. (Source: Fath al-Mughees, page 123)

Shaykh al-Islam Ibn Taymiyah quotes Abd-Allah ibn al-Imaam Ahmad as stating this: I told my father that some people claim that the jinn do not enter the body of a human. He said, O my son, they are lying, for a jinn may speak with the tongue of a person who is lying on his sick-bed (Majmoo' Fataawa Shaykh al-Islam Ibn Taymiyah, 19/12, and vol. 24 of his Fataawa (p. 276, 277)).

Shaykh Ibn Uthaymeen (may Allah have mercy on him) said:

> *"Undoubtedly the jinn can have a harmful effect on humans, and they could even kill them. They may harm a person by throwing stones at him, or by trying to terrify him, and by other things that are proven in the Sunnah or indicated by real events. It was reported that the Messenger (s.a.w.) gave permission to one of his Companions to go to his wife during one of the military campaigns as he was a young man who had recently got married. When he reached his house, he found his wife standing at the door, and he objected to that. She said to him, 'Go inside,' so he went inside and found a snake curled up on the bed. He had a spear with him, so he stabbed it with the spear until it died, and at the same instant as the snake died the man also died. It was not known which of them died first, the snake or the man. When the prophet (s.a.w.) heard of that, he forbade killing the harmless kinds of snakes that are found in houses, apart from those which are maimed or are streaked and malignant.*

> *This indicates that the jinn may attack humans, and that they may harm them, as is known from real-life events. There are numerous reports which indicate that a man may come to a deserted area, and a stone may be thrown at him, but he does not see anybody, or he may hear voices or a rustling sound like the rustling of trees, and other things that may make him feel distressed and scared. A jinn may also enter the body of a human, either because of love or with the intention of harming him, or for some other reason. This is indicated in the aayah mentioned earlier:*

﴿الَّذِينَ يَأْكُلُونَ الرِّبَا لَا يَقُومُونَ إِلَّا كَمَا يَقُومُ الَّذِي يَتَخَبَّطُهُ الشَّيْطَانُ مِنَ الْمَسِّ﴾

'Those who eat Ribaa (interest) will not stand (on the Day of Resurrection) except like the standing of a person beaten by Shaytan (Satan) leading him to insanity' [Surah al-Baqarah 2:275].

In such cases, the jinn may speak from inside of that person and address the one who is reading verses from the Quran over him; the reciter may take a promise from the jinn never to come back, and other things concerning which there are very many reports widespread among the people.

So for protection from the evil of the jinn, a person can recite what is narrated in the Sunnah as being effective in providing protection, such as Aayat al-Kurisy, for if a person recites Aayat al-Kursiy at night, he will continue to have protection from Allah, and no Shaytan will come near him until morning. And Allah is the Protector.

(Majmoo' Fataawa al-Shaykh Ibn Uthaymeen, 1/287-288)

So, the Quran, hadith, and real-life experiences of many people prove that a person may get possessed by jinn.

Another way that shayateen can hurt humans is through their whispers or instilling 'waswas' (doubts) in their minds and hearts. Through this, the devils seek to weaken a person's faith, and create conflicts among people. Allah says in the Quran:

﴿وَإِمَّا يَنزَغَنَّكَ مِنَ الشَّيْطَانِ نَزْغٌ فَاسْتَعِذْ بِاللَّهِ ۚ إِنَّهُ هُوَ السَّمِيعُ الْعَلِيمُ﴾

"And if an evil whisper from Shaytan (Satan) tries to turn you away (O Muhammad) (from doing good), then seek refuge in Allah. Verily, He is the All-Hearer, the All-Knower" [Surah Fussilat, 41:36].

﴿إِنَّ الَّذِينَ اتَّقَوْا إِذَا مَسَّهُمْ طَائِفٌ مِّنَ الشَّيْطَانِ تَذَكَّرُوا فَإِذَا

هُم مُّبْصِرُونَ﴾

Verily, for those who are Al-Muttaqoon (the pious), when an evil thought comes to them from Shaitan (Satan), they remember (Allah), and (indeed) they then see (aright) (Surah Al-Aa'raaf, 7:201).

The prophet (s.a.w.) explained to us about how a Shaytan whispers to a person(s.a.w.):

"The Shaytan comes to one of you and says, 'Who created you?' And he says 'Allah.' Then the Shaytan says, 'Who created Allah?' If that happens to any one of you, let him say, Aamantu Billaahi wa Rusulihi (I believe in Allah and His Messenger). Then that will go away from him." (Narrated by Ahmad, 25671; classed as hasan (sound)byAl-Albaani in Al-Saheehah, 116).

The reality of evil whispers is also proven by the fact that some of the prophet's companions complained to him about the doubts and evil whispers that used to bother them.

Some for example said to him, 'We find in ourselves thoughts that are too terrible to speak of.' He said, 'Are you really having such thoughts?' They said, 'Yes.' He said, 'That is a clear sign of faith' (Narrated by Muslim, 132 from the hadeeth of Abu Hurayrah).

Many scholars have commented that evil whispers and doubts are a sign of faith because Shaytan instills such thoughts only in Muslims' hearts. Al-Nawawi said in his commentary on this hadeeth (prophet's narration): "The prophet's words, 'That is a clear sign of faith' means the fact that thinking of this waswaas as something terrible is a clear sign of faith, for if you dare not utter it and you are so afraid of it and of speaking of it, let alone believing it, this is the sign of one who has achieved perfect faith and who is free of doubt."

Consider the following dua that the prophet (s.a.w.) used to say:

اللَّهُمَّ إِنِّي أَعُوذُ بِكَ مِنَ الْهَدْمِ، وَأَعُوذُ بِكَ مِنَ التَّرَدِّي، وَأَعُوذُ بِكَ مِنَ الْغَرَقِ، وَالْحَرَقِ، وَالْهَرَمِ، وَأَعُوذُ بِكَ مِنْ أَنْ يَتَخَبَّطَنِي الشَّيْطَانُ عِنْدَ الْمَوْتِ

Allahumma innee auudu bika minal-hadm (i), wa auudu bika minat-taraddi, wa auudu bika minal-gharaq (i), wal-harq (i), wal-haram (i), wa auudu bika min ay-yatakhabbaTaniyash-Shaytanu indal-mawt

"O Allah! I seek refuge in You from demolitions. I seek refuge in You from falling down from high places. I seek refuge in You from drowning, burning and old age. I seek refuge in You from Satan's temptations at death" [Source: Sunan Abu-Daawuud # 1552].

Commenting on this dua and hadeeth, al-Manawi said: "[The phrase] 'and I seek refuge with You from being beaten by the Shaytan at the time of death' means, lest he should wrestle with me and play with me, and damage my religious commitment or mental state (at the time of death) by means of his insinuating whispers which cause people to slip or lose their minds. The Shaytan could take control of a person when he is about to depart this world, and misguide him or stop him from repenting…"

In another hadith it was narrated from Ibn Abbaas that a man came to the prophet (s.a.w.) and said, "I think thoughts to myself, which I would rather be burnt to a cinder than speak of them." The prophet (s.a.w.) said, "Praise be to Allah, Who has reduced all his [the Shaytan's] plots to mere whispers" (Narrated by Abu Dawood).

The prophet (s.a.w.) gave us the good news that the believers will not be punished for the doubts and waswaas that cross their hearts and minds. He (s.a.w.) said,

"Allah will forgive my ummah (followers) for any insinuating whispers that may cross their minds, so long as they do not act upon them or speak of them." (Agreed upon).

However, as believers, we are also to ward off these doubts and whispers by reciting Adhkars (Allah's remembrances) and Quranic verses. Seikh Muhammad ibn Saalih Al-Uthaymeen has recommended the following to ward off whispers and doubts:

- *Seek refuge with Allah and give up these thoughts completely, as the prophet (s.a.w.) commanded.*
- *Remember Allah and control yourself and do not continue to think of these whispers.*
- *Occupy yourself with worship and doing good deeds, in obedience to the command of Allah and seeking to please Him. When you devote yourself completely and seriously to worship, you will forget about these whispers, in sha Allah.*
- *Frequently seek refuge with Allah and make dua to free you from these whispers.*

[Source: (Majmoo' Fataawa wa Rasaa'il Fadeelat Al-Shaykh Muhammad ibn Saalih Al-Uthaymeen, vol. 1, p. 57-60)]

It is also confirmed in the two Saheehs from Annas, who reported the story of Safiyyah (prophet's wife) when she came to visit the prophet (s.a.w.) while he was performing I`tikaf, that he went out with her during the night to walk her back to her house. So, two men from the Ansar met him (on the way). When they saw the prophet (s.a.w.), they began walking swiftly. So, the Messenger of Allah (s.a.w.) said,

«عَلَى رِسْلِكُمَا، إِنَّهَا صَفِيَّةُ بِنْتُ حُيَيَ»

(Slow down! This is Safiyyah bint Huyay!) They said, "Glory be to Allah, O Messenger of Allah!" He said,

إِنَّ الشَّيْطَانَ يَجْرِي مِنِ ابْنِ آدَمَ مَجْرَى الدَّمِ، وَإِنِّي خَشِيتُ

أَنْ يَقْذِفَ فِي قُلُوبِكُمَا شَيْئًا، أَوْ قَالَ: شَرًّا

(Verily, Shaytan runs in the Son of Adam like the running of the blood. And verily, I feared that he might cast something into your hearts.)

Another way that Shaytan can hurt humans is through magic. That is explained in the next chapter.

5 The Reality of Sihr (Black Magic)

Sihr (Arabic word for witchcraft) is part of the unseen world where people work with the devils (shayateen) to harm an individual. These acts refer to "magical" effects through the use of incantations and evil practices to cause certain harm to others. The root of the word "sihr" means hidden. It is called so as its practices and effects are hidden. Sahirs (magicians) attempt to bring the desired effects through the repeated use of satanic incantations and practices. Three things about sihr are important to recognize. First, the practice of sihr (witchcraft) does exist and cannot be dismissed as someone's imagination. The Quran and hadith provide numerous references to such satanic practices. Islamic scholars and most people are aware of numerous cases in their daily lives in which people's lives have been adversely affected through such practices. People have been employing the use of sihr ever since the times of Prophet Suleman (a.s.) when its knowledge spread through the devils.

Second, Islamic teachings strictly prohibit the use of sihr in all its forms. The use of sihr and witchcraft is, therefore, considered a grave crime and is *haram* (against Islamic teachings) from all viewpoints and in all situations. As will be discussed further, the use of sihr to even nullify the effects of sihr is also haram and illegal.

Third, the treatment of those who are affected by sihr can only be performed through the use of Quranic verses and Allah's words along with the authentic duas available through the prophet's hadith. The use of any other treatment including that of sihr itself to treat sihr is completely forbidden in Islam.

Sihr is mostly prevalent in areas where *jahliyaa* (ignorance) is widespread and people's jealousy and enmity reaches to such criminal levels that they are willing to use any kind of tactics to harm others. In such situations, magicians (sahirs) say strange incantations and / or perform evil practices such as tying knots on which they blow and pray to the devils (shayaateen) and seek their help in harming people. Similarly, they can prepare evil potions with the intent of giving it to people who they want to be harmed.

As is obvious from the following Quranic verse, magicians sometimes recite evil incantations and blow on objects to make their magic effective:

$$﴿وَمِن شَرِّ النَّفَّاثَاتِ فِي الْعُقَدِ﴾$$

"And (I seek Allah's protection) from the evil of those who practise witchcraft when they blow in the knots" [Surah Al-Falaq, 113:4].

In some cases, sihr is to just create an illusion. The Quran mentions the magicians' power to bewitch people's eyes. Allah says:

$$﴿قَالَ بَلْ أَلْقُوا ۖ فَإِذَا حِبَالُهُمْ وَعِصِيُّهُمْ يُخَيَّلُ إِلَيْهِ مِن$$
$$سِحْرِهِمْ أَنَّهَا تَسْعَىٰ﴾$$

"and their sticks, by their magic, appeared to him as though they moved fast" [Surah Ta-Ha, 20:66].

$$﴿قَالَ أَلْقُوا ۖ فَلَمَّا أَلْقَوْا سَحَرُوا أَعْيُنَ النَّاسِ وَاسْتَرْهَبُوهُمْ$$
$$وَجَاءُوا بِسِحْرٍ عَظِيمٍ﴾$$

"He [Prophet Moosa] said: 'Throw you (first).' So when they threw, they bewitched the eyes of the people, and struck terror into them, and they displayed a great magic" [Surah Al-A'raaf, 7:116].

In other cases, sihr and evil eye can cause serious harm. People have regularly employed the services of evil magicians to rob others of their wealth, sour marital relationships, and to harm them in other ways. Sihr is also commonly performed on women to prevent them from getting married. This is referred to as *sihr Al-ta'teel*. In such cases, marriages don't happen without any real cause and women, who are mostly the victim of such sihr, remain unmarried for no apparent reasons.

Sahirs also work to instill hatred between a husband and his wife. This falls in the other kinds of sihr called Al-*sarf and Al-Atf* that involve creating the desired feelings of hatred or love, by taking inspiration from the devils.

On another extreme level, sihr may also be used to kill people. When discussing different forms of murder, the scholars have mentioned that the person who kills another by means of a kind of sihr or witchcraft should be tried in the same manner as a person who kills by any other means (islamqa.info).

Even Prophet Muhammad (s.a.w.) was affected by sihr and Allah in His wisdom then revealed two surahs (chapters) to rid the effects of the magic that was done on the prophet (s.a.w.). As a result of that incident, the believers were taught to recite the two surahs (Surah Al-Falaq and Surah An-Nas in the Quran) frequently to ward off the effects of sihr [(Source: Majmoo' Fataawaa wa Maqaalaat MutanawwiAh li Samaahat Al-Shaykh Al-Allaamah Abd Al-Azeez ibn Baaz, p. 65)].

5.1 Learning Sihr

Performing sihr or learning sihr is clearly haram (forbidden) in Islam. More than being just an ordinary sin, learning and practicing magic puts one out of the fold of Islam in a state of 'kufr". The following Quranic verses clearly show this. Allah says:

وَاتَّبَعُوا مَا تَتْلُو الشَّيَاطِينُ عَلَى مُلْكِ سُلَيْمَانَ ۖ وَمَا كَفَرَ

سُلَيْمَانُ وَلَٰكِنَّ الشَّيَاطِينَ كَفَرُوا يُعَلِّمُونَ النَّاسَ السِّحْرَ وَمَا

أُنزِلَ عَلَى الْمَلَكَيْنِ بِبَابِلَ هَارُوتَ وَمَارُوتَ ۚ وَمَا يُعَلِّمَانِ مِنْ

أَحَدٍ حَتَّىٰ يَقُولَا إِنَّمَا نَحْنُ فِتْنَةٌ فَلَا تَكْفُرْ ۖ فَيَتَعَلَّمُونَ

مِنْهُمَا مَا يُفَرِّقُونَ بِهِ بَيْنَ الْمَرْءِ وَزَوْجِهِ ۚ وَمَا هُم بِضَارِّينَ بِهِ

مِنْ أَحَدٍ إِلَّا بِإِذْنِ اللَّهِ ۚ وَيَتَعَلَّمُونَ مَا يَضُرُّهُمْ وَلَا يَنفَعُهُمْ

ۚ وَلَقَدْ عَلِمُوا لَمَنِ اشْتَرَاهُ مَا لَهُ فِي الْآخِرَةِ مِنْ خَلَاقٍ ۚ

وَلَبِئْسَ مَا شَرَوْا بِهِ أَنفُسَهُمْ ۚ لَوْ كَانُوا يَعْلَمُونَ

"They followed what the Shayaateen (devils) gave out (falsely of the magic) in the lifetime of Sulaymaan (Solomon). Sulaymaan did not disbelieve, but the Shayaateen (devils) disbelieved, teaching men magic and such things that came down at Babylon to the two angels, Haaroot and Maaroot, but neither of these two (angels) taught anyone (such things) till they had said, 'We are for trial, so disbelieve not (by learning this magic from us).' And from these (angels) people learn that by which they cause separation between man and his wife, but they could not thus harm anyone except by Allah's leave. And they learn that which harms them and profits them not. And indeed they knew that the buyers of it (magic) would have no share in the Hereafter. And how bad indeed was that for which they sold their own selves, if they but knew [Surah Al-Baqarah, 2:102].

If we ponder on the meaning of these verses, we would know that the knowledge of sihr is haram and is a test for mankind.

Sheikh ibn Baaz stated the following about learning the knowledge of witchcraft and sihr:

> *"Learning witchcraft is all kufr, hence Allah stated that the two angels did not teach it to people until they had told them, "We are for trial, so disbelieve not (by learning this magic from us)." Then He says, "but they could not thus harm anyone except by Allah's Leave" so it is known that it is kufr and misguidance, and that the practitioners of witchcraft cannot harm anyone except by Allah's leave. What is meant is His universal qadar (decree) will (i.e., things that He decrees should happen even though He may dislike them), not His religious shar'i will (i.e., that which He prescribes and which pleases Him) – because Allah has not prescribed this and has not given permission for it in His shareeah; rather He has forbidden it and stated that it is kufr and is from the teachings of the devils. And He has stated that whoever buys it – i.e., learns it – will have no share in the Hereafter. This is a serious warning. Then Allah says: "And how bad indeed was that for which they sold their own selves, if they but knew" – what is meant is that they have sold themselves to the devils for this witchcraft. Then Allah says, "And if they had believed and guarded themselves from evil and kept their duty to Allah, far better would have been the reward from their Lord, if they but knew!" – this indicates that learning witchcraft and using it is the opposite of faith and piety. There is no power and no strength except with Allah"* [Majmoo' Fataawa wa Maqaalaat MutanawwiAh li'l-Shaykh Ibn Baaz, 6/371].

5.2 Symptoms of Those Affected by Sihr / Evil Eye

There are no definite or clear symptoms to prove that someone is affected by sihr. However, those who treat such cases indicate the presence of a repetitive behavioral pattern in the persons affected by sihr, evil eye, or jinn possession. These symptoms also vary depending on the severity of the case. In some situations, there may not be any visible symptoms other than what a person may generally experience in life. Also, as mentioned earlier, it should be noted that the presence of these symptoms does not necessarily imply that a person has been affected by sihr or evil eye; rather these symptoms can signal a medical condition as well. A person, therefore, should also seek medical consultation to ensure that such conditions are not ignored.

Islamic scholars have described the following symptoms in those who are afflicted by sihr and jinn possession:

- Reacting strongly (as if shocked and disturbed) or getting repulsed, upon hearing the Quranic verses or any of Allah's reminders

- Fainting, losing consciousness, and experiencing seizures upon hearing Quran recitation

- Experiencing a certain kind of madness or irrational behavior. Allah states in the Quran, *"Those who eat Ribaa [usury / interest] will not stand (on the Day of Resurrection) except like the standing of a person beaten by Shaytan (Satan) leading him to insanity"* *[Surah al-Baqarah, 2:275].*

- When the Quran is recited over the patient, the person speaks in a different voice (that of the devil) and can be heard through the person's body.

- Having frightening dreams and experiencing disturbing sleep patterns

- A change in one's social behavior and disassociating from people and spending time alone

- An unexplained disliking of one's spouse and avoiding the spouse altogether, as Allah tells us in the Quran: *"And from these (angels) people learn that by which they cause separation between a man and his wife..." (Surah Al-Baqarah, 2:102)*

- Getting indulged in strange imaginations

- An unexplained and awkward change in one's behavior

- Developing sudden love or hatred for something or someone

- Showing a variety of physical symptoms without a proper medical explanation

- Having strange hallucinations

- Developing strange marks on the body for no apparent reasons

- Excessive arguments and fights at home without any reason

- Feeling fatigued with no medical explanations

- Repeated hearing of strange noises and seeing apparitions

- Becoming angry for no real reason

- In general, a sudden change in one's medical condition for the worse, with no real medical explanations

- Developing hatred or lack of interest toward Allah's remembrance and reciting the Quran

As mentioned earlier, these symptoms can be due to other conditions as well. Care, therefore, should be taken in diagnosing and treating these problems by consulting both medical professionals along with Islamic scholars.

6 The Reality of "Evil Eye"

An evil eye (*Al-Ain*) refers to a particular look of someone that is focussed on something / someone with jealousy (hasad). One of the definitions provided by scholars is that *"The Arabic word Al-Ain (translated as the evil eye) refers to a condition in which a person harms another with his eye. It begins when the person likes a thing, and then his evil feelings affect it by means of his repeated looking at the object of his jealousy. Allah commanded Prophet Muhammad (s.a.w.) to seek refuge with Him from the envier."* The prophet (s.a.w.) used to seek protection with Allah from the jinn and from the evil eye of human beings, as narrated by Al-Bukhari and Muslim (Zaad Al'Maad).

According to Al-Haafiz Ibn-Hajar, *"The evil eye is a wicked person's look that is loaded with admiration mixed with envy, which harms whatever / whoever is looked at"*. [Source: Ibn Hajar's Fathul-Baari fee Sharh Saheeh Al-Bukhari, No. 10/210.]

The scholars say:

> *Everyone who puts the evil eye on another is envious, but not every envier puts the evil eye on another. The word haasid (envier) is more general in meaning than the word Ain (one who puts the evil eye on another), so seeking refuge with Allah from the one who envies includes seeking refuge with Him from the one who puts the evil eye on another. The evil eye is like an arrow which comes from the soul of the one who envies and the one who puts the evil eye on another towards the one who is envied and on whom the evil eye is put; sometimes it hits him and sometimes it misses. If the target is exposed and unprotected, it will affect him, but if the target is cautious and armed, the arrow will have no effect and may even come back on the one who launched it. (Adapted from Zaad Al-MaAad.)*

Both, the Quran and hadith affirm the existence of the evil eye and the harms it causes. Many people in their everyday lives attest to people's jealousy affecting their health, career and relationships. In a famous hadith in Muslim, Ahmad and Al-Tirmidhi quote from Ibn Abbaas that the prophet (s.a.w.) said:

> *"The evil eye is real and if anything were to overtake the divine decree, it would be the evil eye..." This was classed as saheeh by Al-Tirmidhi, and also by Al-Albaani in Al-Silsilah Al-Saheehah, 1251.*

Allah mentions the reality of evil eye in a number of places in the holy Quran. In one instance, Prophet Yaqub (a.s.) instructed his sons, who were in the prime of their youth, to enter in a gathering of people from different doors, fearing that people's evil eye may hurt them. The fear of Prophet Yaqub from people's jealousy that may have resulted in evil eye, affirms the fact that its effects are really harmful. Allah mentions this in the Quran in the following verse:

$$﴿وَقَالَ يَا بَنِيَّ لَا تَدْخُلُوا مِن بَابٍ وَاحِدٍ وَادْخُلُوا مِنْ أَبْوَابٍ مُّتَفَرِّقَةٍ ۖ وَمَا أُغْنِي عَنكُم مِّنَ اللَّهِ مِن شَيْءٍ ۖ إِنِ الْحُكْمُ إِلَّا لِلَّهِ ۖ عَلَيْهِ تَوَكَّلْتُ ۖ وَعَلَيْهِ فَلْيَتَوَكَّلِ الْمُتَوَكِّلُونَ﴾$$

And he (Yaqub) said: "O my sons! Do not enter by one gate, but enter by different gates, and I cannot avail you against Allah at all. Verily! The decision rests only with Allah. In him, I put my trust and let all those that trust, put their trust in Him" (Surah Yousuf, 12:67).

In another Quranic verse, Allah mentions the following:

﴿وَإِن يَكَادُ الَّذِينَ كَفَرُوا لَيُزْلِقُونَكَ بِأَبْصَارِهِمْ لَمَّا سَمِعُوا الذِّكْرَ وَيَقُولُونَ إِنَّهُ لَمَجْنُونٌ﴾

And verily, those who disbelieve would almost make you slip with their eyes through hatred when they hear the reminder (the Quran), and they say: "Verily, he (Muhammad s.a.w.) is a madman!" (Surah Al-Qalam 68:51)

Ibn Kathir states that the term "slip with their eyes" refers to inflicting an evil eye and this fact further affirms that the effects of evil eye can be harmful (8/201). Commenting on this verse, Ibn Abbaas and others also said: "This means, they cast an evil eye on you with their glances."

Ibn Al-Qayyim stated this in Zaad al-Maad:

"And there is no doubt that Allah, Most Glorified, has created in human bodies and spirits different powers and characteristics and He has created in many of them attributes and qualities which can affect others, so it is not possible for any rational person to reject the effect of some souls on bodies, because that is something which is apparent (to all). And it is not actually the eye which affects a person, but rather the spirit, but because of its strong connection to the eye, the deed has been attributed to it. And the spirit of the envious person is harmful to the person of whom he is envious in a manner which is most clear. For this reason, Allah commanded His Messenger (s.a.w.) to seek refuge from the evil of it.

And the one who emits the evil eye is not dependent upon seeing the object of his envy; indeed, he might even be blind and the thing (which incites his envy) might be described to him. And many of them have their effect through a description, without having seen the object of their envy. So every person from whom Al-Ain is emitted is envious (Hasid), but not every envious person causes Al-Ain, but because envy is more general than it, seeking protection from it means seeking protection from Al-Ain. And it is an arrow which emanates from the soul of the envious one and the one who emits Al-Ain; if it strikes him when he is unprotected, it will affect him, but if he is on his guard and he is armed, it will not affect him and it might even be returned to the one who cast it in like manner. A person might even afflict himself with the evil eye, or he might afflict someone unintentionally by his (evil) nature, and this is the worst kind of evil eye (P-449).

The prophet (s.a.w.) mentioned in a number of hadith about seeking protection from the effects of the evil eye. Ayesha reported that the prophet (s.a.w.) used to tell her to recite ruqyah for protection against the evil eye [as narrated in Al-Saheehayn].

Al-Tirmidhi narrated that Asma bint Umays said: *"O Messenger of Allah, the children of Ja'far have been afflicted by the evil eye, shall we recite ruqyah for them?" He said, "Yes, for if anything were to overtake the divine decree it would be the evil eye."*

In Surah Al-Falaq, Allah asked His servants to seek His protections from the envier's (evil) eye. Allah says,

$$﴿وَمِن شَرِّ حَاسِدٍ إِذَا حَسَدَ﴾$$

"And (I seek protection) from the evil of the envier when he envies" [Surah Al-Falaq, 113:5]

We also know from another hadith that once the prophet (s.a.w.) was travelling towards Makkah, and they stopped at the mountain pass of Al-Kharaar in Al-Jahfah. There, Sahl ibn Haneef, who was a handsome white-skinned man with beautiful skin, did *ghusl* (took a bath). Aamir ibn Rabeeah, one of Banu Adiyy ibn Kaab looked at him and said: "I have never seen such beautiful skin as this, not even the skin of a virgin," and Sahl fell to the ground. They went to the prophet (s.a.w.) and said, "O Messenger of Allah, can you do anything for Sahl, because by Allah, he cannot raise his head." He said, "Do you accuse anyone with regard to him?" They said, "Aamir ibn Rabeeah looked at him." So the prophet (s.a.w.) called Aamir and rebuked him strongly. He said, "Why would one of you kill his brother? If you see something that you like, then pray for blessing for him." [Source: Imam Ahmad (15550), Maalik (1811), Al-Nasaa'i and Ibn Hibbaan narrated from Sahl ibn Haneef]. Later, the prophet (s.a.w.) instructed them to perform the evil eye treatment and Sahl got up and joined the people as there was nothing wrong with him [Classed as saheeh by Al-Albaani in Al-Mishkaat, 4562]. (See chapter 13 for duas and Islamic treatment for those afflicted with evil eye.)

On the basis of the ahaadeeth quoted above and others, a majority of the scholars are of the view that people can indeed be afflicted by the evil eye, and their belief is also supported by the corroborating reports and other evidence in history.

In another hadith, the prophet (s.a.w.) said:

> "Most of those who die among my ummah die because of the will and decree of Allah, and then because of the evil eye." [The author of Nayl Al-Awtaar said that Al-Bazzaar narrated with a hasan isnaad from Jaabir.]

We should also note that evil eye is of two types: (i) of humans and (ii) of the jinn. It has been authentically reported from Umm Salamah that the prophet (s.a.w.) once saw a slave girl in her house and on her face was a *Safah* (a dark spot) and he said:

> "Make incantation for her, for she has been afflicted by An-Nazrah (i.e. the evil eye) [Narrated by Al-Bukhari and Muslim. (Zaad Al'Maad)]

Al-Baghawi said: "Safah means An-Nazrah from the jinn. He (s.a.w.) was saying that she has been afflicted by the evil eye from the jinn, which was more piercing than the points of spears."

As for the symptoms of being affected by the evil eye, Shaykh Abd Al-Azeez Al-Sadhaan said the following:

> "If it does not take the form of a real sickness, then the symptoms may take the following forms: "Headaches that move from one part of the head to another; yellow pallor in the face; sweating and urinating a great deal; weak appetite; tingling, heat or cold in the limbs; palpitations in the heart; pain in the lower back and shoulders; sadness and anxiety; sleeplessness at night; strong reactions due to abnormal fears; a lot of burping, yawning and sighing; withdrawal and love of solitude; apathy and laziness; a tendency to sleep; health problems with no known medical cause."

> These signs or some of them may be present according to the strength of the evil eye or the number of people who put the evil eye on others" [Source: Al-Ruqyah Al-Shar'iyyah (p. 10)].

7 Conditions for Ruqyah Treatment

Scholars have specified that for a ruqyah to be effective, certain conditions are necessary. Sheikh Ibn Uthaymeen said: "Ruqyah is of many types: that which is mentioned in the Sunnah – it is prescribed to use it as ruqyah; that which is *shirk* (associating others with Allah or with His powers) or *bidaah* (innovation) – it is haram to use it as ruqyah; that which is a permissible dua in which there is no shirk or bidaah, but it is not something that was narrated from the prophet (s.a.w.) – it is permissible to use this as ruqyah. Hence the prophet (s.a.w.) said concerning ruqyah: *'There is nothing wrong with it so long as it is not shirk'*" (Source: Fataawa Noor Ala ad-Darb, 6/14.).

Ruqya, therefore, must use Allah's words from the Quran or duas directed to Allah as taught to us by the prophet (s.a.w.). It should be performed by reciting the words of Allah, may He be exalted, or His names and attributes, and they should be recited preferably in Arabic. Ruqyah should be performed with the belief that ruqyah has no effect in and of itself; rather it is only effective by the will of Allah, may He be exalted. Al-Qurtubi said: *Any (ruqyah) that involves reciting the words or names of Allah is permissible; if it is narrated in a report (from the prophet (s.a.w.)) it is mustahabb* (Source: Fath Al-Baari, 10/195.).

In Saheeh Muslim it is narrated that Awf ibn Maalik said: *"We used to recite ruqyahs, and we said: 'O Messenger of Allah, what do you think about that?' He said: 'Recite your ruqyahs to me. There is nothing wrong with a ruqyah that does not involve shirk.'"*

Both the patient and the person treating (raaqi) must believe in their hearts that the treatment comes only from Allah and the words by themselves do not bring any treatment. The focus, therefore, shouldn't be on the mechanics but rather on the belief in Allah alone to be the sole source of treatment.

Sheikh Ibn Baaz stated the following:

أَنْ يُعْتَقَدَ أَنَّ الرُّقْيَةَ لاَ تُؤَثِّرُ بِذَاتِهَا؛ بَلْ بِقُدْرَةِ اللَّهِ تَعَالَى

The belief should be that the ruqyah by itself will not have any effect but by the power of Allah [Source: Fatwa Al-Allama Ibn Baaz 384/2.].

This proves that the idea is not just to go by the mechanics of reciting certain words. Rather, it should be with the belief in the power of Allah's words along with the belief that only Allah can cure ailments. Allah says in the Quran:

﴿وَمَن يَتَوَكَّلْ عَلَى اللَّهِ فَهُوَ حَسْبُهُ﴾

". . . And whosoever puts his trust in Allah, then He will suffice him. . ." [Surah Al-Talaaq, 65:3]

Some people mistakenly think that the effects of sihr can only be warded off by special people. While it is true that some pious scholars may have more effect through their Quran recitation and making dua, in general, this can be done by anyone. Anyone, therefore, can perform ruqyah on themselves or they can have a pious mahram family member recite ruqyah on them. If the one who performs ruqyah does so by reciting general verses of the Quran or general prayers seeking refuge with Allah or other duas for ruqyah, or whatever Allah may inspire him with of saheeh duas that are appropriate to the situation, without restricting it to the specific ruqyahs that have been narrated, there is nothing wrong with that because of the general meaning of the words of the prophet (s.a.w.): *"Whoever among you is able to benefit his brother, let him do so"* (Narrated by Ahmad, 13973; classed as saheeh by Al-Albaani in Saheeh Al-Jaami', 6019).

8 The Forbidden Ways of Treatment and Healing

While Islamic guidelines approve the use of ruqyah and medical sciences for treatment, they also clearly caution against the use of certain other *haram* practices that are common in many communities across the world. Such practices, unfortunately, were not only prevalent during earlier times but are also actively used today. This section covers some of those practices.

8.1 Treatment Using Sihr (Magic)

'Nushrah' is a term that refers to the treatment of sihr using sihr. This is haram and one should never pursue this evil method. The underlying principle of this commandment of Islam is that evil cannot be treated with evil. The prophet (s.a.w.) also strictly forbade using Nushrah. In one of the hadith, when asked about the possibility of using Nushra, he stated: *"This is the work of the Shaytan."*

Clearly, the essence of the prophet's (s.a.w.) instructions is that as sihr is based on the works of the devil and shayateen; therefore, one cannot seek the help of shayateen under any circumstances even when the objective is to nullify the effects of sihr. This is because seeking the help of shayateen pushes one outside the fold of Islam. Thus, only Allah's help should be sought for all treatments of sihr (witchcraft) and evil eye.

On this topic, Al-Shaykh Al-Allaamah Abd Al-Azeez ibn Abd-Allah ibn Baaz stated the following:

> *"Sihr is evil and is kufr. If a sick person is not cured by reading (Quran and dua), then we should note that medicine does not guarantee a cure either, because not every treatment produces the desired result. Allah may delay the*

healing for a long time or the person may die from this sickness. It is not a condition of treatment that the person should be healed. If a person is treated by reading Quran and does not recover, that is not an excuse for turning to sihr, because we are commanded to take only the permissible means and are forbidden to use haram means. The prophet (s.a.w.) said, "O slaves of Allah, seek treatment but do not seek treatment with that which has been forbidden to you." And it was narrated that he (s.a.w.) said: "Allah does not make your healing in that which He has forbidden to you."

All things are in the hand of Allah, may He be glorified. He is the One Who heals whomsoever He wills, and He decrees sickness and death for whomsoever He wills, as He says:

$$\text{﴿وَإِن يَمْسَسْكَ اللَّهُ بِضُرٍّ فَلَا كَاشِفَ لَهُ إِلَّا هُوَ ۖ وَإِن يَمْسَسْكَ بِخَيْرٍ فَهُوَ عَلَىٰ كُلِّ شَيْءٍ قَدِيرٌ﴾}$$

"And if Allah touches you with harm, none can remove it but He, and if He touches you with good, then He is Able to do all things" [Surah Al-AnAam, 6:17].

He also says:

$$\text{﴿وَإِن يَمْسَسْكَ اللَّهُ بِضُرٍّ فَلَا كَاشِفَ لَهُ إِلَّا هُوَ ۖ وَإِن يُرِدْكَ بِخَيْرٍ فَلَا رَادَّ لِفَضْلِهِ ۚ يُصِيبُ بِهِ مَن يَشَاءُ مِنْ عِبَادِهِ﴾}$$

"And if Allah touches you with harm, there is none who can remove it but He; and if He intends any good for

you, there is none who can repel His Favor which He causes to reach whomsoever of His slaves He wills. And He is the Oft-Forgiving, the Most Merciful [Surah Yoonus, 10:107].

So the Muslim must be patient and seek reward with Allah. He must limit himself to the means that Allah has permitted, and beware of that which Allah has forbidden, whilst also believing that the decree of Allah is beneficial and that His command cannot be put back, as Allah says:

$$﴿إِنَّمَا أَمْرُهُ إِذَا أَرَادَ شَيْئًا أَن يَقُولَ لَهُ كُن فَيَكُونُ﴾$$

"Verily, His command, when He intends a thing, is only that He says to it, 'Be!' and it is! [Surah Yaa-Seen, 36:82].

$$﴿وَمَا تَشَاءُونَ إِلَّا أَن يَشَاءَ اللَّهُ رَبُّ الْعَالَمِينَ﴾$$

"And you cannot will unless (it be) that Allah wills the Lord of the Aalameen (mankind, jinn and all that exists) [Surah Al-Takweer, 81:29].

And there are many similar Quranic verses.

[Source: Majmoo' Fataawa wa Maqaalaat MutanawwiAh li Samaahat, vol. 8, p. 112.]

8.2 The Use of Amulets, etc.

Many people use charms and beads around the necks of children or animals, because they claim that it is meant for repelling the evil eye or to fend off an illness. These charms, amulets, etc., are also called Tamimah (also referred to by such names as amulets / taweez / talisman, etc.) for the purpose of healing or preventing problems.

Such acts are strictly prohibited, as they are based on *shirk*, which is the worst form of sins and puts a person out of the fold of Islam. The Messenger of Allah (s.a.w.) forbade such superstitious acts and stated that lucky charms (amulets, taweez, etc.) and similar methods will only intensify the disease and magnify the presence of evil.

An incident from the prophet's traditions sheds light on the reaction of the holy prophet (s.a.w.) upon seeing a person wearing an amulet: *"The Messenger of Allah (s.a.w.) once saw a man wearing an iron ring around his hand and asked him, "What is this?" The man said, "To repel Al-Wahinah," which was a common disease among Arabs during that time. The prophet (s.a.w.) said, "Take it off of your hand, for verily, it will only increase your weakness! If you die while wearing it, you will never attain success.""*

We observe that the Messenger of Allah (s.a.w.) stated in this Hadith that wearing a ring or a lucky charm will not prevent an illness. On the contrary, it will intensify the disease along with the weakness it brings to the body. He also said that if a man died while wearing that ring, he would never attain success. The philosophy behind the prophet's strong dislike of wearing lucky charms is that indirectly, people may be resorting to such useless objects instead of praying to Allah for His help. Such acts may weaken a person's belief in Allah; therefore, one should only pray to Him for his mercy and help.

Once, a group of people came to the Messenger (s.a.w.) to swear their allegiance to embrace Islam and he accepted their Bai'ah (oath of allegiance) except for one man. When they asked the Messenger of Allah about the reason for not accepting his Bai'ah, he said that he did so because that man was wearing a Tamimah (lucky charm). So the man inserted his hand inside his clothing, took the lucky charm out and tore it off. The Messenger then accepted the Bai 'ah from him, saying, *"Whoever wears a Tamimah will have committed shirk."* [Source: (Narrated by Ahmad, 16969)]

We also know that once when Hudhaifah visited a sick person and touched his arm, he found a knot tied around it. He asked him,

"What is this?" The sick man said, "A ruqyah (healer, or lucky charm) that was prescribed to me." Hudhaifah tore the knot and said to him, "If you died while wearing this, I would not have prayed the funeral prayer for you."

It is clear from the prophet's (s.a.w.) ahadith that such a tamimah that neither contains a part of the Quran, nor mentions Allah's name is an act of shirk. Even wearing a lucky charm that contains a part of the Quran or Allah's Names, is also a forbidden act because the prophet (s.a.w.) forbade wearing the Tamimah, regardless of what is written inside it. Moreover, according to many scholars the habit of wearing the latter type of tamimah might give way to *shirk* and people may start writing something other than the holy verses from the Quran. Furthermore, if the holy verses from the Quran are hung around one's neck, it is carried into the bathrooms and dirty places along with the person who is wearing it. Surely, the Quran was not revealed for the purpose of being hung around one's neck, but as a healer for the ills of the hearts. The Quran was not revealed so that one makes Tamimah out of it, or to sell Tamimah that contains parts of it for money, thus acquiring a little sum for selling Allah's Words [Source: Taken from Ahadith Al-Minbar, by Shaikh Abdul-Aziz bin Abdullah bin Hasan AlShaikh, p. 59].

Consider the statement of the scholars (Fataawa al-Lajnah al-Daa'imah, 1/212) which states: *"The scholars are agreed that it is haram to wear amulets if they contain anything other than Quran, but they differed concerning those which do contain Quran. Some of them said that wearing these is permitted, and others said that it is not permitted. The view that it is not permitted is more likely to be correct because of the general meaning of the ahaadeeth, and in order to prevent means of shirk"* (Shaykh Abd al-Azeez ibn Baaz, Shaykh Abd-Allah ibn Ghadyaan, Shaykh Abd-Allah ibn Qaood).

Sheikh Muhammed Salih Al-Munajjid states the following:

"Undoubtedly not allowing that [wearing amulets with Quranic verses] is a safer precaution to prevent means that lead to wrong beliefs, especially in our own times. If most of the Sahaabah and Taabi'een regarded it as makrooh in

those noble times when the faith in their hearts was greater than a mountain, then regarding it as makrooh in these times of trials and tribulations is more appropriate and is more on the safe side."

Shaykh Ibn Uthaymeen said:

"So long as there is no proof that a thing is a means (to an end) – either according to Islam or natural, physical laws – then it is a kind of minor shirk. That includes, for example, charms and amulets that are said to ward off the evil eye, and the like, because this is deciding that something is a means to an end when Allah has not created it to be such. Thus he is deciding about something being a means to an end, which is something that is only for Allah to decide. Hence this is like an act of shirk" [Source: Majmoo' Fataawa Ibn Uthaymeen, 10/787].

We should remind ourselves the basic principle that only Allah has all matters in His hand. He says in the Quran:

﴿قُلْ مَن يَكْلَؤُكُم بِاللَّيْلِ وَالنَّهَارِ مِنَ الرَّحْمَٰنِ ۗ بَلْ هُمْ عَن ذِكْرِ رَبِّهِم مُّعْرِضُونَ﴾

"Say: "Who can guard and protect you in the night or in the day from the (punishment of the) Most Gracious (Allah)?" Nay, but they turn away from the remembrance of their Lord." (Surah Al-Anbiya, 21:42).

8.3 Using Strange Methods and Rituals

As mentioned earlier, the power to heal lies in the words of Allah and in Allah's Will alone. Some people instead use strange rituals that have no bearing in the Quran or hadith. Such rituals (use of fire, circling, reciting strange words, etc.) are mere witchcraft and are devilish in nature and have no connection with Islamic treatment or ruqyah. As was mentioned earlier, using any form of treatment that is against Islamic guidelines can instead cause more harm than good. None of the methods used should involve any shirk, which as discussed earlier not only nullifies the treatment but has the potential to push both the patient and raaqi out of the folds of Islam.

9 The Power and Blessings of the Quran

Since most of the spiritual treatment relies on the use of Quranic verses for treatment, it is vital to review the blessings of the Quran and its power to bring about positive changes in a Muslim's life. This section reviews various Quranic verses about the Quran, Ahadeeth (Prophet's Saying) and sayings of the salaf (pious people that followed the prophet) on the majesty of the Quran, and the great virtues of reading and following its commandments.

Allah says in the Quran:

﴿أَوَلَمْ يَكْفِهِمْ أَنَّا أَنْزَلْنَا عَلَيْكَ الْكِتَابَ يُتْلَى عَلَيْهِمْ إِنَّ فِي ذَلِكَ لَرَحْمَةً وَذِكْرَى لِقَوْمٍ يُؤْمِنُونَ﴾

Is it not sufficient for them that We have sent down to you the Book (the Quran) which is recited to them? Verily, herein is mercy and a reminder (or an admonition) for a people who believe (Quran, Surah Ankaboot, 29:51).

About the treatment of various illnesses from the Quran, Ibn Al-Qayyim stated in Zaa'd Al-Maa'd the following (4/352):

فَمَنْ لَمْ يَشْفِهِ الْقُرْآنُ فَلَا شَفَاهُ اللّهُ وَمَنْ لَمْ يَكْفِهِ فَلَا كَفَاهُ اللّهُ

"Whosoever is not cured by the Quran, there is no cure for him and whosoever is not content by it, Allah will not ever make him content."

To begin with, there are many verses in the Quran itself that underscore the majesty of Allah's verses and the Quran itself.

Allah says:

﴿قُل لَّئِنِ اجْتَمَعَتِ الْإِنسُ وَالْجِنُّ عَلَىٰ أَن يَأْتُوا بِمِثْلِ هَٰذَا الْقُرْآنِ لَا يَأْتُونَ بِمِثْلِهِ وَلَوْ كَانَ بَعْضُهُمْ لِبَعْضٍ ظَهِيرًا﴾

"If the mankind and the jinn were together to produce the like of this Quran, they could not produce the like thereof, even if they helped one another" [Quran Al-Israa, 17:88].

﴿لَوْ أَنزَلْنَا هَٰذَا الْقُرْآنَ عَلَىٰ جَبَلٍ لَّرَأَيْتَهُ خَاشِعًا مُّتَصَدِّعًا مِّنْ خَشْيَةِ اللَّهِ ۚ وَتِلْكَ الْأَمْثَالُ نَضْرِبُهَا لِلنَّاسِ لَعَلَّهُمْ يَتَفَكَّرُونَ﴾

"Had We sent down this Quran on a mountain, you would surely have seen it humbling itself and rending asunder by the fear of Allah. Such are the parables which We put forward to mankind that they may reflect" [Surah Al-Hashr, 59:21].

﴿ذَٰلِكَ الْكِتَابُ لَا رَيْبَ ۛ فِيهِ ۛ هُدًى لِّلْمُتَّقِينَ﴾

"This is the Book (the Quran), whereof there is no doubt, a guidance to those who are Al-Muttaqoon [the pious] [Surah Al-Baqarah, 2:2].

A Musilm's status is raised by the Quran – the more he recites and follows its commandments and makes the Quran an integral part of his or her life, the more Allah elevates his or her status in this life and in the hereafter.

> Saheeh Muslim mentions a story where some men came to question Umar ibn Al-Khattaab during his khilaafah about the leadership of Makkah. They asked, "Who do you use to govern Makkah?" He said, "Ibn Abzaa." They asked, "And who is Ibn Abzaa?" Umar replied, "A freed slave from those we freed." They remarked, "You left a freed slave in charge of the people of the Valley (the noble tribes of the Quraysh)?" So he answered them, "Verily he is a reader of the Book of Allah and is knowledgeable about the obligations of the Muslims. Haven't you heard the statement of your Messenger: "Verily Allah raises some people by this Book and lowers others by it."

Narrated Abu Musa: The prophet said,

> The example of a believer who recites the Quran is that of a citron (a citrus fruit) which is good in taste and good in smell. And the believer who does not recite the quran is like a date which has a good taste but no smell. And the example of an impious person who recites the Quran is that of Ar-Rihana (an aromatic plant) which smells good but is bitter in taste. And the example of an impious person who does not recite the Quran is that of a colocynth which is bitter in taste and has no smell" (Book #93, Hadith # 649).

9.1 The Healing Power of the Quran

Allah revealed the Quran as the final message of truth for the entire mankind. As Allah mentions in the Quran, its verses can heal all types of diseases, whether spiritual or physical. Al-Allaamah Muhammad Al-Ameen Al-Shanqeeti says:

"The fact that it is a healing includes the heart and all its diseases (i.e., spiritual diseases), such as doubt, hypocrisy and so on, as well as healing for physical diseases if it is used in ruqya, as is indicated by the story of the one who did ruqyah for the man who had been stung by a scorpion by reciting Al-Faatihah." [Adwa' Al-Bayaan, 3/253]

Allah says:

﴿وَنُنَزِّلُ مِنَ الْقُرْآنِ مَا هُوَ شِفَاءٌ وَرَحْمَةٌ لِلْمُؤْمِنِينَ وَلَا يَزِيدُ الظَّالِمِينَ إِلَّا خَسَارًا﴾

And We send down of the Quran that which is a healing and a mercy to those who believe (in Islamic monotheism and act on it), and it increases the Zaalimoon (polytheists and wrongdoers) nothing but loss" [Surah Al-Isra, 17:82].

﴿يَا أَيُّهَا النَّاسُ قَدْ جَاءَتْكُمْ مَوْعِظَةٌ مِنْ رَبِّكُمْ وَشِفَاءٌ لِمَا فِي الصُّدُورِ وَهُدًى وَرَحْمَةٌ لِلْمُؤْمِنِينَ﴾

"O mankind! There has come to you a good advice from your Lord (i.e. the Quran, ordering all that is good and forbidding all that is evil), and a healing for that (disease of ignorance, doubt, hypocrisy and differences, etc.) in your breasts – a guidance and a mercy (explaining lawful and unlawful things, etc.) for the believers (Quran, Surah Yunus: 57)."

Ibn Al-Qayyim (may Allah have mercy on him) said:

"We and others have tried this on many occasions and we have seen that it works in ways that physical remedies do

not. Indeed we now regard physical medicine as the doctors regard folk medicine. This is in accordance with the law of divine wisdom, not contrary to it, but the causes of healing are many and varied. When the heart is in contact with the Lord of the Worlds, the creator of the disease and the remedy, the controller of nature who directs it as He wills, He has other remedies apart from the remedies that are sought by the heart that is far away from Him and that turns away from Him. It is known that when a person's spirits are high and his body is in good shape, they cooperate in warding off disease and suppressing it, so if a person is in high spirits and physical good shape, he finds comfort in being close to his Creator, loving Him, enjoying remembrance of Him (dhikr), devoting all his strength and power for His sake and focusing on Him, seeking His help, putting his trust in Him; how can anyone deny that this is the greatest medicine or that this spiritual power gives him the means to ward off pain and defeat it completely? No one would deny this but the most ignorant of people, those who are farthest away from Allah and the most hard-hearted and unaware of human nature."

It was narrated that Aaishah (may Allah be pleased with her) said:

When the Messenger of Allah (s.a.w.) was ill, he would recite Al- Mu'wadaitain over himself and spit drily. When his pain grew intense, I recited over him and wiped him with his own hand, seeking its barakah (blessing)." Narrated by Al-Bukhaari, 4728; Muslim, 2192 (Al-Mi'wadhatayn are the last two surahs of the Quran – Surah Al-Falaq and Surah Al-nas.)

9.2 Treating non-Muslims with the Quran

We find through a number of hadith that non-Muslims have also been treated with Quranic verses. However, in such cases, the reciter of the Quranic verses was a Muslim. In a well known hadith that was reported in Al-Bukhaari (2276) and Muslim (2201), Abu Sa'eed Al-Khudri (may Allah be pleased with him) said:

"A group of the companions of the prophet (s.a.w.) set out on a journey and traveled until they stopped in (the land of) one of the Arab tribes. They asked them for hospitality but they refused to welcome them. The chief of that tribe was stung by a scorpion (or snake) and they tried everything but nothing helped them. Some of them said, 'Why don't you go to those people who are camped (near us), maybe you will find something with them.' So they went to them and said, 'O people, our chief has been stung by a scorpion and we have tried everything but nothing helped him. Can any of you do anything?' One of them said, 'Yes, by Allah, I will recite ruqyah for him, but by Allah we asked you for hospitality and you did not welcome us, so I will not recite ruqyah for you until you give us something in return.' Then they agreed upon a flock of sheep. Then he went and spat drily and recited over him Al-hamdu Lillaahi Rabb il-Aalameen [Surah Al-Faatihah]. [The chief] got up as if he was released from a chain and started walking, and there were no signs of sickness on him. They paid them what they agreed to pay. Some of them (i.e. the companions) then suggested to divide their earnings among themselves, but the one who performed the ruqyah said, 'Do not divide them until we go to the prophet (s.a.w.) and tell him what happened, then wait and see what he tells us to do.' So they went to the Messenger of Allah (s.a.w.) and told him what had happened. The Messenger of Allah (s.a.w.) asked, 'How did you know that it (Al-Faatihah) is a ruqyah?' Then he added,

'You have done the right thing…" (narrated by Al-Bukhaari, 2156; Muslim, 2201).

It says in Al-Mawsooah Al-Fiqhiyyah (13/34): *"There is no difference of opinion among the fuqaha' that it is permissible for a Muslim to treat a non-Muslim with ruqya, and they quoted as evidence the hadeeth of Abu Sa'eed Al-Khudri quoted above. The point here is that the tribe with whom they halted and from whom they sought hospitality, but who refused to give them any hospitality, were non-Muslims, but the prophet (s.a.w.) did not object to him doing that."*

10 The Power of Remembrance of Allah

Shaytan's goal is to misguide the believers and to inflict harm on them from whatever channels are available to him. However, we should protect ourselves from Shaytan and his tactics and his whispers by remembering Allah at all times. In a popular hadith narrated by Al-Tirmidhi (2863), Allah commanded Yahya ibn Zakariyya (peace be upon him) to tell the Children of Israel to do five things, including the following:

> *"I command you to remember Allah, for the likeness of that is that of a man whose enemy comes after him, until he comes to a strong fortress where he protects himself from him. Similarly, a person cannot protect himself against the Shaytan except by remembering Allah." [Classed as saheeh by Al-Albaani in Saheeh Al-Tirmdihi (2863)]*

Ibn al-Qayyim said: Shaykh al-Islam (Ibn-e-Taymiyyah) used to regard this hadeeth highly, and I heard that he used to say: "The evidence for its being sound is quite clear." (Source: al-Waabil al-Sayyib, 60.)

Dhikr of Allah means: fulfilling our obligations of His worship, performing voluntary prayers, remembering Allah other than during the obligatory and voluntary prayer, reciting the Quran, and fasting. Such acts will enable us to get closer to Allah and to stay away from Shaytan because Shaytan easily attacks such people who do not follow their religious duties.

Ibn Al-Qayyim mentions in his book "Medicine of the prophet" the following:

The heart becomes well when it acquires knowledge of its Lord and Creator and in His names, attributes, actions and commandments. The heart also becomes well when it prefers acquiring Allah's pleasure and prefers what He likes, all the while avoiding His prohibitions and what might lead to His displeasure.

Remembance of Allah makes one soul and heart stronger, which can psychologically aid in healing the ailments of the body.

Ibn Al-Qayyim also stated in the same book:

"...whenever the soul and the heart become stronger spiritually, they will cooperate to defeat the illness."

A Muslim, therefore, should constantly fight the Satan by remembering Allah, and by engaging in the Quranic recitations, and through daily adhkars, prayers, and fasting. A person who constantly remembers Allah through different forms of prayers is kept safe from the harms of Satan. Allah says in the Quran:

﴿فَقَاتِلُوا أَوْلِيَاءَ الشَّيْطَانِ ۖ إِنَّ كَيْدَ الشَّيْطَانِ كَانَ ضَعِيفًا﴾

"... So fight you against the friends of Shaytan (Satan); ever feeble indeed is the plot of Shaytan (Satan)" [Surah al-Nisa, 4:76].

We should remember that although Shaytan will stay away from people who are righteous, pious and who remember Allah at all times, yet he will try his tactics on those who he thinks will slip easily. He will, therefore, continue his attacks on such people through not just satanic whispers but also through other means and in some cases, it may harm them physically.

It is recorded in Tafsir Ibn Kathir that Imam Ahmad recorded that Ibn Abbas said, "A man came to the prophet and said, `O Messenger of

Allah! Sometimes I say things to myself that I would rather fall from the sky than say (aloud openly).' The prophet said,

اللهُ أَكْبَرُ، اللهُ أَكْبَرُ الْحَمْدُ لِلهِ الَّذِي رَدَّ كَيْدَهُ إِلَى لُوَسْوَسَةِ

(Allah is Most Great! Allah is Most Great! All praise is due to Allah Who sent his (Shaytan's) plot back as only a whisper.)" Abu Dawud and An-Nasa'i also recorded this Hadith.

When we remember Allah, He remembers us and this protects us in times of calamity and difficulty. Let us reflect on the following verse and some of the Ahadith of the prophet to see the benefits of remembering Allah.

﴿فَاذْكُرُونِي أَذْكُرْكُمْ وَاشْكُرُوا لِي وَلَا تَكْفُرُونِ﴾

"Therefore remember Me (by praying, glorifying), I will remember you, and be grateful to Me (for My countless Favors on you) and never be ungrateful to Me" (Surah Al-Baqarah, 2:152).

In another hadith, Ibn 'Abbaas said that the prophet (s.a.w.) said, "I was behind the Messenger of Allah (s.a.w.) one day and he said:

يَا غُلَامُ إِنِّي أُعَلِّمُكَ كَلِمَاتٍ احْفَظْ اللَّهَ يَحْفَظْكَ احْفَظْ اللَّهَ

تَجِدْهُ تُجَاهَكَ إِذَا سَأَلْتَ فَاسْأَلْ اللَّهَ وَإِذَا اسْتَعَنْتَ فَاسْتَعِنْ

بِاللَّهِ وَاعْلَمْ أَنَّ الأمة لَوْ اجْتَمَعَتْ عَلَى أَنْ يَنْفَعُوكَ بِشَيْءٍ

لَمْ يَنْفَعُوكَ إِلاَّ بِشَيْءٍ قَدْ كَتَبَهُ اللَّهُ لَكَ وَلَوْ اجْتَمَعُوا عَلَى أَنْ

يَضُرُّوكَ بِشَيْءٍ لَمْ يَضُرُّوكَ إِلاَّ بِشَيْءٍ قَدْ كَتَبَهُ اللَّهُ عَلَيْكَ
رُفِعَتْ الْأَقْلَامُ وَجَفَّتْ الصُّحُفُ

"O boy, I shall teach you some words. Be mindful of Allah and He will take care of you. Be mindful of Allah and He will protect you. If you ask then ask of Allah, and if you seek help then seek help from Allah. Know that if the nation were to gather together to benefit you in some way, they would not benefit you except in something that Allah has decreed for you, and if they were to gather together to harm you in some way, they would not harm you except in something that Allah has decreed for you. The pens have been lifted and the pages have dried." (Classed as saheeh by al-Albaani in Saheeh al-Tirmidhi 2516, Saheeh Al Tirmidhi 309/2.)

There is no better protection for us than Allah (our Creator) remembering us, His slaves. So, the more we remember Allah, the more He remembers us and the more He would protect us from the harms of Shaytan. According to a hadith Narrated by Abu Hurairah, the prophet said,

"Allah says, I am just as My slave thinks I am, (i.e. I am Able to do for him what he thinks I can do for him) and I am with him if he remembers Me. If he remembers Me in himself, I too, remember him in Myself; and if he remembers Me in a group of people, I remember him in a group that is better than them; and if he comes one span nearer to Me, I go one cubit nearer to him; and if he comes one cubit nearer to Me, I go a distance of two outstretched arms nearer to him; and if he comes to Me walking, I go to him running (Saheeh Al-Bukhâri, Vol.9, Hadîth No.502).

Ibn Taymiyyah said:

> "...one should persist in remembering Allah in general, the best of which is Laa ilaaha ill-Allah. There may be some situations where certain kinds of dhikr are preferable, such as saying Subhaana Allah wa'l-hamdu-Lillaah wa Allahu akbar wa laa hawla wa laa quwwata illa Billaah.
>
> Moreover, one should realize that everything that the tongue utters or the heart imagines that may bring one closer to Allah, such as seeking knowledge or teaching, enjoining what is good and forbidding what is evil, is a kind of dhikr or remembering Allah. Hence the one who occupies himself in the pursuit of beneficial knowledge after performing the obligatory duties, or who joins a gathering in order to learn or teach, which Allah and His Messenger have called fiqh or understanding, is also doing something which is one of the best forms of remembering Allah (dhikr)." [Source: al-Wasiyyah al-Jaami'ah li Khayr al-Dunya wa'l-Aakhirah]

It was reported from Abu Hurayrah that the prophet (s.a.w.) said:

> "There are seven whom Allah will shade with His shade on the day when there will be no shade except His: (1) the just ruler; (2) a young man who grows up worshipping his Lord; (3) a man whose heart is attached to the mosque; (4) two men who love one another for the sake of Allah and meet and part on that basis; (5) a man who is called by a woman of rank and beauty but he tells her that 'I fear Allah'; (6) a man who gives in charity and conceals it to such an extent that his left hand does not know what his right hand gives; and (7) a man who remembers Allah when he is alone, and his eyes fill up" (Agreed upon, and narrated by al-Bukhaari, no. 620; Muslim, no. 1712; and others).

The prophet (s.a.w.) said:

"When I say 'Subhaan Allah, wa'l-hamdu Lillah, wa laa ilaah ill-Allah, wa Allahu akbar (Glory be to Allah, praise be to Allah, there is no god except Allah, and Allah is Most Great)', this is more beloved to me than all that the sun rises upon" *(Narrated by Muslim)*

سُبْحَانَ اللَّهِ ، وَالْحَمْدُ لِلَّهِ ، وَلَا إِلَهَ إِلَّا اللَّهُ ، وَاللَّهُ أَكْبَرُ

From the above quoted Ahadeeth, we can see that inculcating the habit of constant remembrance of Allah in our everyday lives can ward off our physical and spiritual ailments and can help us in the recovery process, as Allah's mercy is with those who constantly remember Him.

11 The Power of Dua

Trials, tribulations and challenges are part of every person's life. However, to counter that, Allah has provided us a very powerful tool – and that is the tool of dua or asking Allah for His help and mercy, whenever we need it. Whether we need His help for healing our illnesses or for making things better in times of calamity; we should actively rely on the power of dua to get Allah's help. The prophet (s.a.w.) said about making dua:

الدُّعَاءُ يَنْفَعُ مِمَّا نَزَلَ وَمِمَّا لَمْ يَنْزِلْ، فَعَلَيْكُمْ عِبَادَ اللَّهِ بالدُّعاء

The dua benefits for (clamities) that have already happened and those that are yet to happen; so keep praying O slaves of Allah.

Source: Thirmidi 3548, Wa-al Hakim 670/1, Wa-Ahmad braqm 22044, Wa Hasan Al-Bani.

He (s.a.w.) also said,

لاَ يَرُدُّ القَضَاءَ إلاّ الدُّعاءُ، وَلاَ يَزِيدُ فِي الْعُمُرِ إلاّ الْبِرُّ

"Nothing turns away the decree but dua (to Allah), and nothing adds to ones life (age) but good deeds."

Source: Al-Hakim 670/1, Thirmidi 2139, wa-Hasan Al-Bani in: Series of Ahadith Saheeh 76/1, 154.

The following are some of the prophet's sayings about making dua to Allah and the enormous potential it holds to help us ask for forgiveness and other things:

- Prophet (s.a.w.) said: *"The dua of any one of you will be answered so long as he does not seek to hasten it, and does not say, 'I made dua' but I had no answer"* (Narrated by al-Bukhaari, 5865; Muslim, 2735, from the hadeeth of Abu Hurayrah).

- The hadeeth which was narrated by al-Tirmidhi from Abu Hurayrahsays: "The Messenger of Allah (s.a.w.) said: *'There is no man who prays to Allah and makes dua to Him, and does not receive a response. Either it will be hastened for him in this world, or it will be stored up for him in the Hereafter, so long as he does not pray for something sinful, or to cut the ties of kinship, or seek a speedy response.'* They said, 'O Messenger of Allah, what does seeking a speedy response mean?' He said, 'Saying, 'I prayed to my Lord and He did not answer me.'" (Al-Tirmidhi, 3859; classed as saheeh by al-Albaani in Saheeh al-Tirmidhi, 852).

- Some people follow practices that are not sanctioned by the Quran or Hadith such as repeating some of Allah's names a certain times. A number of scholars have said that "The words mentioned in the question are phrases that are narrated in the Quran and Sunnah, but saying that they must be repeated [so many] number of times is an innovated new practice which should not be followed. Rather we should mention them during our duas and address Allah by all His beautiful names, without singling out some names or stating that they should be recited a certain number of times or at certain times, making that up ourselves. We should adhere to what was narrated in shareeah concerning certain times, places or situations connected to a particular dua; if no such details were narrated in shareeah then we should not make them up ourselves because that is encroaching upon the rights of prophethood.

- The hadeeth says: *"One of you may be answered so long as he is not hasty and says, 'I said dua but I got no response.'"* Narrated by al-Bukhaari, 6340; Muslim, 2735.

- In Saheeh Muslim (2736) we find this: "A man's (duas) may be answered so long as it does not involve sin or severing the ties of kinship or hastening." It was said: "O Messenger of Allah, what does hastening mean?" He said: "When he says, 'I made dua but I did not see any response,' so he gets discouraged and stops making dua."

- The dua should not involve sin or severing of the ties of kinship, as stated in the hadeeth quoted above: "A man's (duas) may be answered so long as it does not involve sin or severing the ties of kinship …"

- According to the hadeeth of Abu Hurayrah: *"Make dua to Allah when you are certain of a response."* Narrated by al-Tirmidhi; classed as hasan by al-Albaani in Saheeh al-Jaami', 245.

- The prophet (s.a.w.) said: "Know that Allah does not answer a dua from a distracted heart." Narrated by al-Tirmidhi, 3479; classed as hasan by al-Albaani in Saheeh al-Jaami', 245.

- In the hadeeth it says: The prophet (s.a.w.) mentioned the man who undertakes a lengthy journey and is disheveled and covered with dust, and he stretches his hands towards heaven saying, 'O Lord, O Lord,' when his food is haram, his drink is haram, his clothes are haram. He is nourished with haram, so how can he be granted a response?

PART II

RUQYAH (VERSES AND DUAs) FROM QURAN AND SUNNAH

12 Blessings of Certain Quranic Verses from Hadith

As demonstrated earlier, the entire Quran is shifa and healing for all types of ailments and diseases. Any surah or part of the Quran can be used with the specific intention of healing (or making any other supplication or dua) and reciting those verses. However, the prophet (s.a.w.) had highlighted specific blessings of certain surahs and verses of the Quran. In addition to that, scholars have also noted the healing effects of some other Quranic verses. For example, for the treatment of black magic, many have recommended recitation of Quranic verses that include references to black magic. They have also recommended recitation of Quranic verses that allude to Allah's power to nullify Satanic tactics and other   evil plans.

Although there are authentic ahadeeth regarding the rewards and benefits of reciting certain Quranic surahs, unfortunately there are several fabricated ahadeeth that highlight the benefits of other surahs. Therefore, not all ahadeeth highlighting the benefits of reciting surahs are authentic, even though some of those ahadeeth mention a chain of narrators. Many scholars have proved the weakness of the narration chain of those ahadeeth. Scholars have noted that, *"Many ahaadeeth were fabricated about the virtues of various surahs of the Quran. The fabricators' intention was to encourage people to read the Quran and devote themselves to that, and they claimed that they were doing good thereby. But their intention was misguided because that is undoubtedly subject to the stern warning contained in the words of the prophet (s.a.w.): "Whoever tells a lie about me deliberately, let him take his place in Hell." (Narrated by Al-Bukhaari, 10; Muslim, 4.) It makes no difference whether the lie is intended for good or for evil. (Source: islamqa.info).*

The next few sections highlight the benefits and blessings of certain Quranic verses that are supported by authentic narrations and references from the prophet's hadith.

12.1 Blessings of Surah Al-Faatihah

Surah Al-Faatihah has special blessings as was specifically mentioned by the prophet (s.a.w.). In one of the hadith the prophet (s.a.w.) told us that it was the greatest surah of the Quran. This surah can be used to ward off evil and for general healing.

The reference to this surah is made in other parts of the Quran as well. Consider the following verse of Surah Al-Hijr:

﴿وَلَقَدْ آتَيْنَاكَ سَبْعًا مِّنَ الْمَثَانِي وَالْقُرْآنَ الْعَظِيمَ﴾

"And indeed, We have bestowed upon you seven of Al-Mathani (the seven repeatedly recited Verses), (i.e. Surah Al-Faatiha) and the Grand Quran" (Surah Al-Hijr, 15:87).

Abu Sa'îd bin Al-Mu'alla says:

> *While I was praying in the mosque, Allah's Messenger called me but I did not respond to him. Later I said, "O Allah's Messenger, I was praying." He said, "Didn't Allah say – Answer Allah (by obeying Him) and His Messenger when he calls you?" He then said to me, "I will teach you a surah which is the greatest Surah in the Quran, before you leave the mosque." Then he got hold of my hand, and when he intended to leave (the mosque), I said to him, "Didn't you say to me, "I will teach you a surah which is the greatest surah in the Quran?" He said, "Al-Hamdu lillahi Rabbil-'alamîn [i.e. all the praises and thanks be to Allah, the Lord of the 'Alamîn (mankind, jinn and all that exists)], Surat Al-Faatihah which is As-Sab' Al-Mathani (i.e. the seven repeatedly recited*

Verses) and the Grand Quran which has been given to me"
(Saheeh Al-Bukhari, Vol.6, Hadith No. 1).

As mentioned in earlier chapters that the prophet (s.a.w.) told us that Surah Al-Faatihah is a great ruqyah for the treatment of ones ailments. Surah Al-Faatihah is the first chapter of the Quran and must be recited in every prayer. According to 'Ubadah bin As-Samit, Allah's Messenger said:

"Whoever does not recite Surat Al-Faatihah in his prayer, his prayer is invalid (Saheeh Al-Bukhari, Vol.1, Hadîth No. 723).

Surah Al-Faatihah is, therefore, used to ward off many evils such as sihr and evil eye, and for the treatment of physical ailments as well. Many miracles have been observed and reported when this surah is recited by righteous and pious people over the affected individuals with the conviction that the power to heal lies only in the hands of Allah and not in the words that are spoken or in those who speak it. This taqwa and sincerity is essential in the healing of people. While reciting this surah, it should be repeated several times and over many days if necessary.

Sunan Abu Dawood and Ahmed also mention Surah Al-Faatihah as one of the Surahs for ruqyah treatment.

وَأَعْظَمُ الْعِلاَجِ الرُّقْيَةُ بِفَاتِحَةِ الْكِتَابِ ...

"··· And one of the biggest ruqyah treatments is with Surah Al-Faatihah."

Source: Sunan Abu Dawood 14-13/14 # 3896, wa Ahmad 210/5 # 21835, wa sahaha albani fi silsilah alahadith al saheeh #2028.

12.2 The Blessings of Surah Al-Baqarah

Surah Al-Baqarah is the longest surah of the Quran and the prophet (s.a.w.) told us that its recitation in a house keeps the Satan away.

As most of the spiritual ailments such as evil eye, jinn possession, and black magic are satanic in nature, keeping Satan away can help both in the treatment of such conditions and as a preventive measure. Abu Hurayrah reports that the Messenger of Allah (s.a.w.) said: *"Do not make your houses like graves, for the Shaytan runs away from a house in which Soorat al-Baqarah is recited"* *(narrated by Muslim, 780).*

12.3 Blessings of Aayat al-Kursiy

Another Quranic verse that is used for ruqyah and general protection is Ayat-ul-Kursi (Quranic verse related to Allah's throne, which is verse 255 of Surah Al-Bqarah). The Quranic verse is an integral part of the basic ruqyah treatment and is used not only for the treatment of evil eye and black magic, but for general and comprehensive protection as well.

Abu Hurayrah said:

> *The Messenger of Allah (s.a.w.) put me in charge of guarding the zakaah of Ramadaan. Someone came to me and started grabbing (taking illegally) handfuls of the food. I took hold of him and said, 'I will take you to the Messenger of Allah (s.a.w.).' He said, 'I will teach you some words by means of which Allah will benefit you.' I said, 'What are they?' He said, 'When you go to your bed, recite this aayah: "Allah! Laa ilaaha illa Huwa (none has the right to be worshipped but He), Al-Hayyul-Qayyoom (the Ever Living, the One Who sustains and protects all that exists)…" [Surah al-Baqarah, 2:255]. Then Allah will appoint a guard for you who will stay with you and no Shaytan (devil) will come near you until morning.' The Messenger of Allah (s.a.w.) asked me, 'What did your prisoner do last night?' I said, 'O Messenger of Allah, he taught me something, and claimed that Allah would benefit me by it.' He said, 'What was it?' I said, 'He taught me to recite Aayat al-Kursiy when I go to bed, and said that no Shaytan would come near me until*

morning, and that Allah would appoint a guard for me who would stay with me.' The prophet (s.a.w.) said, 'He told you the truth, although he is an inveterate liar. That was the Shaytan' [narrated by al-Bukhaari, 3101; Muslim, 505].

12.4 The Blessings of Last Verses of Surah Al-Baqarah

The last verses of Surah Al-Baqarah are one of the most memorized and recited Quranic verses among Muslims and that is for a good reason. Consider the saying of the prophet (s.a.w.) about the last verses of the Surah.

"Whoever recites the last two verses of Surat al-Baqarah at night, it will suffice him'" (According to Abu Masood al-Ansaari and narrated by al-Bukhaari, 4723; Muslim, 807).

The Prophet (s.a.w.) also said the following:

"Allah inscribed a book two thousand years before He created the heavens and the earth, from which the last two verses of Surat al-Baqarah were revealed. If they are recited for three nights, no Shaytan (devil) will remain in the house) (narrated by al-Tirmidhi, 2882). This hadeeth was classed as saheeh by al-Albaani in Saheeh al-Jaami' (1799).

12.5 The Importance of Mu'wadaitain

"Mu'wadaitain" is an Arabic word that refers to the last two surahs of the Quran, namely **Surah Al-Falaq** and **Surah An-Naas**. Prophet's ahadith clearly tell us that these two surahs were revealed to seek protection from various types of evils. Ibn Al-Qayyim said that *"the effectiveness of these surahs is great to repel magic, evil eye, and the rest of the evils and the need for a slave to seek Allah's protection from these two surahs is greater than his need for self, eating, driking, and wearing dress"* (Al-Fawwaid, 2/426).

According to tafsir ibn Kathir, Abu Saeed reported that the Messenger of Allah (s.a.w.) used to seek protection against the evil eyes of the jinns and mankind. But when the Mu'wadaitain were revealed, he used them (for protection) and abandoned all else besides them (narrated in At-Tirmidhi, An-Nasa'i and Ibn Majah).

Abu Saeed al-Khudri said: "The Messenger of Allah (s.a.w.) used to seek refuge with Allah from the jinn and from the evil eye until the Mu'wadaitain were revealed, and when they were revealed he started to recite them and not anything else" (narrated by al-Tirmidhi, 2058; he said it is hasan ghareeb. Also narrated by al-Nasaa'i, 5494; Ibn Maajah, 3511).

There is another hadith narrated by Abdullah bin Khabeeb who said that, "we got out once on a rainy night and it was very dark and we looked for the prophet (s.a.w.) to pray for us and then we found him and he said 'Did you pray?' and I didn't say anyting. Then he said, 'Say' but I didn't say anything. Then he said, 'Say' but again I didn't say anything. Then he said, 'Say' So, I said, 'What should I say?' He said, 'Qul Hoo wAllahu Ahad and Muwaidaitain when you enter the evening and when you wake up in the morning three times and it will protect you from everything'" (Tirmidhee # 3575), Aby Daud (# 5084).

12.6 The Blessings of Surah Al-Mulk

The prophet (s.a.w.) highlighted certain benefits of Surah Al-Mulk as well. Abu Hurayrah reports that the prophet (s.a.w.) said:

There is a surah of the Quran containing thirty verses which have interceded for a man until he was forgiven. It is the surah Tabaarak alladhi bi yadihi'l-mulk (narrated by Al-Tirmidhi, 2891; Ahmad, 7634; Abu Dawood, 1400; Ibn Maajah, 3786). This hadeeth was classed as hasan by Al-Tirmidhi and by Al-Albaani in Saheeh Al-Tirmidhi, 3/6.

13 Ruqyah from Quran and Hadith Used for Treatment

This chapter includes essential ruqyah that can be used for the treatment of various ailments. Unless otherwise specified, the Quranic verses can be recited for the treatment of all forms of ailments as long as the reciter has the right intention. As for the duas that are included from the hadith, the meanings of duas can be used to choose the right dua for the right condition. For example, the duas that make reference to seeking Allah's protection from evil eye should be used for the treatment (or prevention) of evil eye. Similarly, duas that have reference to seeking Allah's help to relieve one from various forms of pain can be used for that purpose and so on.

The next two sections also highlight the essential ruqyah from Quran and hadith that should be recited for all situations and ailments. Additional Quranic verses and duas follow the essential ruqyah.

13.1 Essential Ruqyah from Quran

Scholars have recommended that for a short ruqyah in treating sihr or other spiritual ailments, the following verses should be used. The verses can be recited directly in the ear of the person, or can be recited over water which is then poured over the person who is affected by sihr or suspected of having sihr. Other methods that are followed by the scholars include reciting the verses and then blowing drily on the patient. This set of Qranic verses is the core in every ruqyah treatment and, therefore, every Muslim should not only memorize these verses but also inculcate the daily habit of reciting them.

1. Surah Al-Faatiha,
2. Surah Al-Baqarah (Verses 1 – 5)
3. Surah Al-Baqarah (Verse 255) (Aayat Al-Kursiy)
4. Surah Al-Baqarah (Verses 284 – 286)
5. Surah Yousuf (Second part of Verse 64)
6. Surah Al-Kafiroon
7. Surah Al-Ikhlas
8. Al- Mu'wadaitain (Surah Al-Falaq and Surah An-Naass)

Again, it is important that a person recites these regularly, with sincerity and faith in their power, and believing that all trials and healing are only from Allah.

The following are all the verses of the short ruqyah along with their trasnslation:

Surah Al-Faatihah	*Verses 1 – 7*	سُورَةُ الفَاتِحَةِ

In the name of Allah, the most, merciful, the most beneficient	بِسْمِ اللهِ الرَّحْمَنِ الرَّحِيمِ
All the praises and thanks be to Allah, the Lord of the Alamin (mankind, jinn and all that exists).	الْحَمْدُ لِلَّهِ رَبِّ الْعَالَمِينَ
The Most Gracious, the Most Merciful	الرَّحْمَنِ الرَّحِيمِ
The Only Owner (and the Only Ruling Judge) of the Day of Recompense (i.e. the Day of Resurrection)	مَالِكِ يَوْمِ الدِّينِ
You (Alone) we worship, and You (Alone) we ask for help (for each and everything).	إِيَّاكَ نَعْبُدُ وَإِيَّاكَ نَسْتَعِينُ

Guide us to the straight path.	اهدِنَا الصِّرَاطَ الْمُسْتَقِيمَ
The way of those on whom You have bestowed Your Grace, not (the way) of those who earned Your anger (i.e. those who knew the truth, but did not follow it) nor of those who went astray (i.e. those who did not follow the truth out of ignorance and error).	صِرَاطَ الَّذِينَ أَنْعَمْتَ عَلَيْهِمْ غَيْرِ الْمَغْضُوبِ عَلَيْهِمْ وَلَا الضَّالِّينَ

Surah Al-Baqara	**Verses 1 – 5**	سورة البقرة

Alif-Lam-Mim [These letters are one of the miracles of the Quran and none but Allah knows their meanings.]	الم
This is the Book (the Quran), whereof there is no doubt, a guidance to those who are Al-Muttaqun [the pious believers of Islamic monotheism who fear Allah much (abstain from all kinds of sins and evil deeds which He has forbidden) and love Allah much (perform all kinds of good deeds which He has ordained).	ذَلِكَ الْكِتَابُ لاَ رَيْبَ فِيهِ هُدًى لِّلْمُتَّقِينَ
Who believe in the Ghaib and perform As-Salat (Iqamat-as-Salat), and spend out of what We have provided for them [i.e. give Zakat, spend on themselves, their parents, their children, their wives, etc., and	الَّذِينَ يُؤْمِنُونَ بِالْغَيْبِ وَيُقِيمُونَ الصَّلاةَ وَمِمَّا رَزَقْنَاهُمْ يُنفِقُونَ

also give charity to the poor and also in Allah's Cause - Jihad].	
And who believe in (the Quran and the Sunnah) which has been sent down (revealed) to you (O Muhammad (s.a.w.)) and in that which was sent down before you [the Taurat (Torah) and the Injeel (Gospel), etc.] and they believe with certainty in the Hereafter (Resurrection, recompense of their good and bad deeds, Paradise and Hell).	وَالَّذِينَ يُؤْمِنُونَ بِمَا أُنزِلَ إِلَيْكَ وَمَا أُنزِلَ مِن قَبْلِكَ وَبِالآخِرَةِ هُمْ يُوقِنُونَ
They are on (true) guidance from their Lord, and they are the successful.	أُوْلَئِكَ عَلَى هُدًى مِّن رَّبِّهِمْ وَأُوْلَئِكَ هُمُ الْمُفْلِحُونَ

Surah Al-Baqara	Verse 255	سورة البقرة

Allah! La ilaha illa Huwa (none has the right to be worshipped but He), Al-Hayyul-Qayyum (the Ever Living, the One Who sustains and protects all that exists). Neither slumber nor sleep overtakes Him. To Him belongs whatever is in the heavens and whatever is on the earth. Who is he that can intercede with Him except with His Permission? He knows what happens to them (His creatures) in this world, and what will	اللَّهُ لاَ إِلَهَ إِلاَّ هُوَ الْحَيُّ الْقَيُّومُ لاَ تَأْخُذُهُ سِنَةٌ وَلاَ نَوْمٌ لَّهُ مَا فِي السَّمَاوَاتِ وَمَا فِي الأَرْضِ مَن ذَا الَّذِي يَشْفَعُ عِندَهُ إِلاَّ بِإِذْنِهِ يَعْلَمُ مَا بَيْنَ أَيْدِيهِمْ وَمَا خَلْفَهُمْ

happen to them in the Hereafter. And they will never compass anything of His Knowledge except that which He wills. His Kursi extends over the heavens and the earth, and He feels no fatigue in guarding and preserving them. And He is the Most High, the Most Great.	وَلاَ يُحِيطُونَ بِشَيْءٍ مِّنْ عِلْمِهِ إِلاَّ بِمَا شَاء وَسِعَ كُرْسِيُّهُ السَّمَاوَاتِ وَالأَرْضَ وَلاَ يَؤُودُهُ حِفْظُهُمَا وَهُوَ الْعَلِيُّ الْعَظِيمُ

Surah Al-Baqara	**Verses 284-286**	سورة البقرة

To Allah belong all that is in the heavens and all that is on the earth, and whether you disclose what is in your own selves or conceal it, Allah will call you to account for it. Then He forgives whom He wills and punishes whom He wills. And Allah is Able to do all things.	لِّلَّهِ مَا فِي السَّمَاوَاتِ وَمَا فِي الأَرْضِ وَإِن تُبْدُواْ مَا فِي أَنفُسِكُمْ أَوْ تُخْفُوهُ يُحَاسِبْكُم بِهِ اللَّهُ فَيَغْفِرُ لِمَن يَشَاء وَيُعَذِّبُ مَن يَشَاء وَاللَّهُ عَلَى كُلِّ شَيْءٍ قَدِيرٌ
The Messenger (Muhammad (s.a.w.)) believes in what has been sent down to him from his Lord, and (so do) the believers. Each one believes in Allah, His Angels, His Books, and His Messengers. (They say), "We make no distinction between one another of His Messengers" - and they say, "We hear, and we obey. (We seek) Your	آمَنَ الرَّسُولُ بِمَا أُنزِلَ إِلَيْهِ مِن رَّبِّهِ وَالْمُؤْمِنُونَ كُلٌّ آمَنَ بِاللَّهِ وَمَلآئِكَتِهِ وَكُتُبِهِ وَرُسُلِهِ لاَ نُفَرِّقُ بَيْنَ أَحَدٍ مِّن رُّسُلِهِ وَقَالُواْ سَمِعْنَا

Forgiveness, our Lord, and to You is the return (of all)."	وَأَطَعْنَا غُفْرَانَكَ رَبَّنَا وَإِلَيْكَ الْمَصِيرُ
Allah burdens not a person beyond his scope. He gets reward for that (good) which he has earned, and he is punished for that (evil) which he has earned. "Our Lord! Punish us not if we forget or fall into error, our Lord! Lay not on us a burden like that which You did lay on those before us (Jews and Christians); our Lord! Put not on us a burden greater than we have strength to bear. Pardon us and grant us Forgiveness. Have mercy on us. You are our Maula (Patron, Supporter and Protector, etc.) and give us victory over the disbelieving people."	لَا يُكَلِّفُ اللَّهُ نَفْسًا إِلاَّ وُسْعَهَا لَهَا مَا كَسَبَتْ وَعَلَيْهَا مَا اكْتَسَبَتْ رَبَّنَا لَا تُؤَاخِذْنَا إِن نَّسِينَا أَوْ أَخْطَأْنَا رَبَّنَا وَلَا تَحْمِلْ عَلَيْنَا إِصْرًا كَمَا حَمَلْتَهُ عَلَى الَّذِينَ مِن قَبْلِنَا رَبَّنَا وَلاَ تُحَمِّلْنَا مَا لَا طَاقَةَ لَنَا بِهِ وَاعْفُ عَنَّا وَاغْفِرْ لَنَا وَارْحَمْنَا أَنتَ مَوْلَانَا فَانصُرْنَا عَلَى الْقَوْمِ الْكَافِرِينَ

Surah Yousuf	**Verse 64**	سورة يوسف

"... But Allah is the Best to guard, and He is the Most Merciful of those who show mercy."	فَاللَّهُ خَيْرٌ حَافِظًا ۖ وَهُوَ أَرْحَمُ الرَّاحِمِينَ

| Surah Al-Kafiroon | Verses 1 – 6 | سورة الكافرون |

Say: (O Muhammad (s.a.w.) to these Mushrikun and Kafirun): "O Al-Kafirun (disbelievers in Allah, in His Oneness, in His Angels, in His Books, in His Messengers, in the Day of Resurrection, and in Al-Qadar)!	قُلْ يَا أَيُّهَا الْكَافِرُونَ
I worship not that which you worship.	لَا أَعْبُدُ مَا تَعْبُدُونَ
Nor will you worship that which I worship.	وَلَا أَنتُمْ عَابِدُونَ مَا أَعْبُدُ
And I shall not worship that which you are worshipping.	وَلَا أَنَا عَابِدٌ مَّا عَبَدتُّمْ
Nor will you worship that which I worship.	وَلَا أَنتُمْ عَابِدُونَ مَا أَعْبُدُ
To you be your religion, and to me my religion (Islamic monotheism).	لَكُمْ دِينُكُمْ وَلِيَ دِينِ

| Surah Al-Ikhlas | Verses 1 – 4 | سورة الإخلاص |

| Say (O Muhammad (s.a.w.)): "He is Allah, (the) One." | قُلْ هُوَ اللَّهُ أَحَد |

Allah-us-Samad (السيد الذي يصمد إليه في الحاجات) [Allah the Self-Sufficient Master, Whom all creatures need, (He neither eats nor drinks)]	اللَّهُ الصَّمَدُ
He begets not, nor was He begotten.	لَمْ يَلِدْ وَلَمْ يُولَد
And there is none co-equal or comparable unto Him.	وَلَمْ يَكُن لَّهُ كُفُوًا أَحَدٌ

Surah Al-Falaq	**Verses 1 – 5**	سورة الفلق

Say: I seek refuge with (Allah), the Lord of the daybreak,	قُلْ أَعُوذُ بِرَبِّ الْفَلَقِ
From the evil of what He has created,	مِن شَرِّ مَا خَلَقَ
And from the evil of the darkening (night) as it comes with its darkness; (or the moon as it sets or goes away),	وَمِن شَرِّ غَاسِقٍ إِذَا وَقَبَ
And from the evil of those who practise witchcraft when they blow in the knots,	وَمِن شَرِّ النَّفَّاثَاتِ فِي الْعُقَدِ
And from the evil of the envier when he envies.	وَمِن شَرِّ حَاسِدٍ إِذَا حَسَدَ

Surah An-Nas	Verses 1 – 6	سورة الناس

Say: I seek refuge with (Allah) the Lord of mankind,	قُلْ أَعُوذُ بِرَبِّ النَّاسِ
The King of mankind -	مَلِكِ النَّاسِ
The Ilah (God) of mankind,	إِلَهِ النَّاسِ
From the evil of the whisperer (devil who whispers evil in the hearts of men) who withdraws (from his whispering in one's heart after one remembers Allah)	مِن شَرِّ الْوَسْوَاسِ الْخَنَّاسِ
Who whispers in the breasts of mankind	الَّذِي يُوَسْوِسُ فِي صُدُورِ النَّاسِ
Of jinn and men.	مِنَ الْجِنَّةِ وَالنَّاسِ

13.2 Essential Dua from Hadith

The following duas are taken from authentic hadith of the prophet. These duas should be recited as part of the ruqyah treatment. This section includes those duas that are part of most ruqyh treatment.

More duas are included in later sections of this chapter. They can be used as part of a more extensive ruqyah treatment.

This marks the beginning of the ruyah treatment and one should recite it 3 times.

بِسْمِ اللَّهِ

Bismillah

"In the name of Allah"

أَعُوذُ بِاللَّهِ السَّمِيعِ الْعَلِيمِ مِنْ الشَّيْطَانِ الرَّجِيمِ مِنْ هَمْزِهِ وَنَفْخِهِ وَنَفْثِهِ

A'oodhu Billaah hiss-samee' il-'aleem minash-Shaytaan ir-rajeem, min-hamzihi, wa-nafkhihi-wa-nafthihi.

"I seek refuge in Allah, the All-Hearing, All-Knowing, from Satan, the outcast, and from his whispers, his blowing and his Nafth."

Source: Sunan Abu-Daawuud, Hadith No. 775 and No. 764. & Sunan Attermidhiy, Hadith No.242.

أَعُوذُ بِكَلِمَاتِ اللَّهِ التَّامَّةِ مِنْ كُلِّ شَيْطَانٍ وَهَامَّةٍ وَمِنْ كُلِّ عَيْنٍ لامَّةٍ

A'oodhu Bikalimaatil-laahit-taammaati-min kulli-shaytanin wa haammatin-, wa-min-kulli-aiynin-laammah.

"I seek refuge in Allah's perfect words from all devils and insects and from all envious eyes."

Source: Saheeh Al-Bukhari, hadith No. 3371.

With regard to the meaning of *laammah*, Al-Khattaabi said: "What is meant here is every disease or harm that a person may suffer such as insanity or mental disturbance."

أَعُوذُ بِكَلِمَاتِ اللَّهِ التَّامَّاتِ كلهن مِنْ شَرِّ مَا خَلَقَ

A'oodhu Bikalimaatil-laahit-taammati-kullahunna, min-sharri-maa-khalaqa.

"I seek refuge in all of Allah's perfect Words from the evil of what He has created."

Source: Saheeh Muslim, Hadith No. 2708. & Musnad Al-Imam Ahmad, Hadith No. 5/364.

It was narrated that Abu Hurayrah said: A man came to the prophet (s.a.w.) and said, "O Messenger of Allah, I am suffering because of a scorpion that stung me yesterday." He said, *"If you had said in the evening, 'A'oodhu bi kalimaat Allah hil-taammah min sharri ma khalaqa (I seek refuge in the perfect words of Allah from the evil of that which He has created),' it would not have harmed you"* .

In a related hadith, Khawlah bint Hakeem Al-Salamiyyah said: "I heard the prophet (s.a.w.) say: "Whoever makes a stop in some place, then says, 'A'oodhu bi kalimaat Allah il-taammah min sharri ma khalaqa (I seek refuge in the perfect words of Allah from the evil of that which He has created),' nothing will harm him until he moves on from that place" (narrated by Muslim, 2708).

بِسْمِ اللَّهِ الَّذِي لَا يَضُرُّ مَعَ اسْمِهِ شَيْءٌ فِي الْأَرْضِ وَلَا فِي السَّمَاءِ وَهُوَ السَّمِيعُ الْعَلِيمُ

Bismillaahil-laathee laa yadhurru ma'a ismihi shay'un-fil ardhi wa laa fis samaai wa Huwas Samee ul- Aleem.

"In the name of Allah, with Whose name nothing in the heavens or the earth can cause any harm, and He is the All-Hearing, All-Knowing."

Source: Sunan Abu-Daawuud, Hadith No. 5088.

بِسْمِ اللَّهِ أَرْقِيكَ ، مُنْ كُلِّ شَيْءٍ يُؤْذِيكَ ، وَمِنْ شَرِّ كُلِّ حَاسِدٍ وَنَفْسٍ ، اللَّهُ يَشْفِيكَ ، بِسْمِ اللَّهِ أَرْقِيكَ

"Bismillaahi arqeeka, min kulli shay'in yu'dheeka, wa min sharri kulli haasidin wa Nafsin Allahu yashfeek, Bismillaahi arqeek

"In the name of Allah I perform ruqyah for you, from everything that is harming you, from the evil of every soul or envious eye may Allah heal you, in the name of Allah I perform ruqyah for you."

Source: Saheeh Muslim, Hadith No. 2186.

بِسْمِ اللَّهِ

أَعُوذُ بِاللَّهِ وَقُدْرَتِهِ مِنْ شَرِّ مَا أَجِدُ وَأُحَاذِرُ

Bismillahi, Aoodhu-billahi wa-qudraatihi-minn-sharri-maa-ajidoo-wa-uhaaziroo.

"I seek refuge in Allah and His might, from the evil of what I find and fear."

Source: Saheeh Muslim, Hadith No. 222. & Sunan Attermidhiy, Hadith No. 3588.

Note: Say Bismillah three times and the dua that follows it above seven times.

أَسْأَلُ اللهَ العَظِيمَ ، رَبَّ العَرْشِ العَظِيمِ ، أَنْ يَشْفِيَكَ

As'al-ullah-al-Azeem rabbi-l-arshil-azeem ann-yashfik (a)

"I pray to Allah, the Magnificent, Lord of the Glorious Throne, to grant your healing."

Source: Sunan Abu-Daawuud, Hadith No. 3106. & Sunan Attermidhiy, Hadith No. 2083. & Musnad Al-Imam Ahmad, Hadith No. 1/239.

اللَّهُمَّ أَذْهِبْ الْبَأْسَ رَبَّ النَّاسِ ، وَاشْفِ أَنْتَ الشَّافِي ، لَا شِفَاءَ إِلَّا شِفَاؤُكَ شِفَاءً لَا يُغَادِرُ سَقَمًا

"Allah-humma adhhib il-ba's, Rabb Al-naas, washfi anta Al-Shaafi laa shifaaA illa shifaa'uka shifaaAn laa yughaadiru saqaman"

"O Allah, Lord of mankind! Remove our suffering. Heal us as You are the healer, and none can heal but You. I beg You to bring about healing that leaves behind no ailment."

Source: Saheeh Al-Bukhari, Hadith No. 5675. & Saheeh Muslim, Hadith No. 2191.

❖❖❖❖❖

اللَّهُمَّ اشْفِ عَبْدَكَ وَصَدِّقْ رَسُولَ

Allahumma-ashafee- abdakaa,wa-saddiq-rasool.

"O Allah, I beg You to grant healing to Your slave, as testimony of trust in Your Messenger."

Source: Sunan Attermidhiy, Hadith No. 2084.

❖❖❖❖❖

اللهُمَّ بَارِكْ عَلَيْهِ، وَأَذْهِبْ عَنْهُ حَرَّ الْعَيْنِ وَبَرْدَهَا وَوَصَبَهَا

Allahumma Baarik alaihee, wa-ad-hib-an'hoo harra-al-aiynee wa-barda'haa wa-wa-saba'aa-haa.

"O Allah, I beg You to grant him Your blessings, to rid him of the evil eye's heat, cold and aches."

Source: Musnad Al-Imam Ahmad, Hadith No. 3/411. & Ibn Al-Atheer's Annihaayah, No. 5/116.

اللَّهُمَّ إِنَّا نَسْأَلُكَ مِنْ خَيْرِ مَا سَأَلَكَ مِنْهُ نَبِيُّكَ مُحَمَّدٌ صلى الله عليه وسلم وَنَعُوذُ بِكَ مِنْ شَرِّ مَا اسْتَعَاذَ مِنْهُ نَبِيُّكَ مُحَمَّدٌ صلى الله عليه وسلم وَأَنْتَ الْمُسْتَعَانُ، وَعَلَيْكَ الْبَلَاغُ، وَلَا حَوْلَ وَلَا قُوَّةَ إِلَّا بِاللَّهِ

Allahumma inna Nas'aluka min-khairee-maa-sa'aaluka-minhoo-nabiyooka-Muhammadun (sallaAllah alaihi wasallam) wa-naoo'dhubika-min-sharri-maa-astaadha minhoo-nabiyooka-Muhammadun (sallaAllah alaihi wasallam) wa-antal-musta'aanoo, wa-alaikal-balaaghoo, wa-la-howla-wa-laquwata-illah-billaah.

"O Allah, we beg You to grant us good as Your Prophet Muhammad begged of You, and we seek refuge in You, from evil as Your Prophet Muhammad sought in You. You are the One whose help is sought, and the One that answers prayers. There is no help or power except from Allah."

Source: Sunan Attermidhiy, Hadith No. 3521.

لَا إِلَهَ إِلَّا اللَّهُ الْعَظِيمُ الْحَلِيمُ، لَا إِلَهَ إِلَّا اللَّهُ رَبُّ الْعَرْشِ الْعَظِيمِ، لَا إِلَهَ إِلَّا اللَّهُ رَبُّ السَّمَوَاتِ، وَرَبُّ الْأَرْضِ، وَرَبُّ الْعَرْشِ الْكَرِيمِ

Laa illaha illal-laah-ul-azeem-ul-haleem, laa illaha illal-laahu rabbul-arshil-azeem, laa illaha illal-laahu rabbus-samawat, wa rabbul-arD, wa-rabbul-arshil-Kareem

"There is no god but Allah, the Magnificent, the forbearing; there is no god but Allah, Lord of the heavens and the earth, and Lord of the Glorious Throne."

Source: Saheeh Al-Bukhari, Hadith No. 6345. & Saheeh Muslim, Hadith No. 2730. & Musnad Al-Imaam Ahmad, Hadiths No. 1/91.

رَبَّنَا اللَّهُ الذِي فِي السَّمَاءِ ، تَقَدَّسَ اسمُكَ ، أَمرُكَ فِي السَّمَاءِ وَالأَرْضِ ، كَمَا رَحمَتُكَ فِي السَّمَاءِ فَاجْعَلْ رَحْمَتَكَ فِي الأَرْضِ ، اغْفِر لَنَا حَوْبَنَا وَخَطَايَانَا ، أَنتَ رَبُّ الطَّيِّبِينَ ، أَنزِلْ رَحْمَةً مِن رَحمَتِكَ ، وَشِفَاءً مِن شِفَائِكَ عَلَى هَذَا الوَجَعِ ، فَيَبرَأَ

Rabbuna-Allahu-laazi fiss-sama-ee, taqaddas(a)-asmuk(a), amruk(a) fiss-samaa-ee wal-ardi, kama rahmatuk(a) fiss-samaa-ee faj'al-rahmatak(a) fil-ard, ighfirlana, hao-bana, wa-khata-yana, anta rabbul-tayyibeen(a), anzil rahmatan min rahmatik(a) wa shifaa-an, min shifaa-ika ala haadal-waja', fayabra-aa

"O our Lord, Allah, You are in Heaven; holy be Your name. Your command reigns supreme in the heavens and on the earth. As Your mercy is in the heavens, have Your mercy on the earth. Forgive our sins. You are the Lord of the good. Send down of Your mercy and healing unto this ailment to cure it."

Source: Sunan Abu-Daawuud, Hadith No. 3892. & Musnad Al-Imam Ahmad, Hadith No. 6/21. & Ibn Al-Qayyim's Zaad Al-Mee'aad, No. 3/141.

اللَّهُمَّ صَلِّ عَلَى مُحَمَّدٍ وَعَلَى آلِ مُحَمَّدٍ كَمَا صَلَّيْتَ عَلَى إِبْرَاهِيمَ وَعَلَى آلِ إِبْرَاهِيمَ. إِنَّكَ حَمِيدٌ مَجِيدٌ اللَّهُمَّ بَارِكْ عَلَى مُحَمَّدٍ، وَعَلَى آلِ مُحَمَّدٍ كَمَا بَارَكْتَ عَلَى إِبْرَاهِيمَ وَعَلَى آلِ إِبْرَاهِيمَ. إِنَّكَ حَمِيدٌ مَجِيدٌ

Allahumma Salli Alla Muhammadiwo Wa Alla-Aale-Muhammadin Kamaa Sallaita Ala Ibraahima Wa-Alla Aale Ibraahima Inn'naka-Hammeedum-Majeed. Allahumma Baarik Alla Muhammadiwo Wa-Ala Aale Muhammadin Kama Baarakta Ala Ibraahima-Wa-Alla Aale Ibraahima Inn'naka –hammedum-Majeed

"O Allah, pray for Muhammad and the family of Muhammad, as You have prayed for Ibraheem and the family of Ibraheem. You are praiseworthy and gloryworthy. O Allah! Bless Muhammad and the family of Muhammad, as You have blessed Ibraheem and the family of Ibraheem, in all the worlds. You are praiseworthy and gloryworthy."

Source: Saheeh Al-Bukhari, Hadith No. 3370. & Saheeh Muslim, Hadith No. 406.

13.3 More Duas for Treatment

أَعُوذُ بِوَجْهِ اللهِ الْكَرِيمِ، وَبِكَلِمَاتِ اللهِ التَّامَّاتِ، اللَّاتِي لَا يُجَاوِزُهُنَّ

بَرٌّ وَلَا فَاجِرٌ، مِنْ شَرِّ مَا يَنْزِلُ مِنَ السَّمَاءِ وَشَرِّ مَا يَعْرُجُ فِيهَا،

وَشَرِّ مَا ذَرَأَ فِي الأَرْضِ وَشَرِّ مَا يَخْرُجُ مِنْهَا، وَمِنْ فِتَنِ اللَّيْلِ

وَالنَّهَارِ، وِمِنْ طَوَارِقِ اللَّيْلِ وَالنَّهَارِ، إِلَّا طَارِقاً يَطْرُقُ بِخَيْرٍ يَارَحْمنُ

A'oodhu Biwajhi-hilkareem,wa-bikalimaatil-laahit-taammaati-llati-laa-yujaawizuhunna-barru-wa-laa-faajirr,min-sharri-maa-yanzilu-minass-samaa'ee-wa-sharri-maa-ya'ruju-feeha,wa-sharri-maa-zara'aa-fee-il-ardi-wa-sharri-maa-yakh'ruju-minha-wa- min-fitanil-laili-wan-nahaari,wa-min-tawaariqil-laili-wann-nahaari-illa-taariqan-yatrukoo-bikhaiyrin,yaa- Rahman.

"I seek refuge in Allah by Allah's Perfect Face and by His Perfect Words, which cannot be surpassed by the righteous or the profligate, from the evil of whatever comes down from heaven and whatever goes up to it, from the evil of whatever goes into the earth and whatever comes out of it, from the trials of night and day and from the knocking disasters of night and day, except a knocker bearing good. O You, the Merciful."

Source: Musnad Ahmad # 3/419

بِسْمِ اللَّهِ أَعُوذُ بِكَلِمَاتِ اللَّهِ التَّامَّاتِ مِنْ غَضَبِهِ وَعِقَابِهِ وَشَرِّ عِبَادِهِ وَمِنْ هَمَزَاتِ الشَّيَاطِينِ وَأَنْ يَحْضُرُونِ

Bismillahi,   A'oodhu-bikalimaatilaahit-taammaati-min-ghadhbihi-wa-iqaabihi-wa-sharri-ibaadihi,   wa-min-hamaazati-shayaateeni,   wa-unn-yahdhuroon.

"In the name of Allah, I seek refuge in Allah's perfect words, from His wrath and punishment, from the evil of His slaves, and from Satan's whispers and presence."

Source: Sunan Abu-Daawuud, Hadith No. 3893.

أَعُوذُ بِاللَّهِ الْعَظِيمِ وَبِوَجْهِهِ الْكَرِيمِ وَسُلْطَانِهِ الْقَدِيمِ مِنَ الشَّيْطَانِ الرَّجِيمِ

A'oodhu Billahil-Azeem, wa-bi-wajhi-hil-Kareem, wa-sultaani-hil-qadeem, minash- Shaytaanir -rajeem.

"By Allah's glorious face and His eternal power, I seek refuge in Allah, the magnificent, from Satan, the outcast."

Source: Sunan Abu-Daawuud, Hadith No. 466. & Al-Albaani's Saheeh Abu-Daawuud, Hadith No. 441.

بِسْمِ اللَّهِ يُبْرِيكَ، وَمِنْ كُلِّ دَاءٍ يَشْفِيكَ، وَمِنْ شَرِّ حَاسِدٍ إِذَا حَسَدَ، وَمِنْ شَرِّ كُلِّ ذِي عَيْنٍ

"Bismillahi Yubreek, wa min kulli daa-in yashfeek, wa min sharri-haasidin izha hasad, wa min sharri kulli zee aynin"

"In the name of Allah, may He grant you healing; may He cure you of all diseases, of the evil of envious ones when they envy, and of the evil eye."

Source: Saheeh Muslim, Hadith No. 2185.

بِسْمِ اللَّهِ تُرْبَةُ أَرْضِنَا بِرِيقَةِ بَعْضِنَا يُشْفَى سَقِيمُنَا بِإِذْنِ رَبِّنَا

Bismillahi-turbatu-ardina, bireeqati-ba'adina, yushfaa saqeemuna, bi-izni-rabbinna.

"In the name of Allah, with the earth of our land and the saliva of some of us, the ill amongst us will be healed by Allah's permission."

Source: Saheeh Al-Bukhari, Hadhith No. 5745. & Saheeh Muslim, Hadith No. 2194.

بِسْمِ اللَّهِ الْكَبِيرِ أَعُوذُ بِاللَّهِ الْعَظِيمِ مِنْ شَرِّ كُلِّ عِرْقٍ نَعَّارٍ وَمِنْ شَرِّ حَرِّ النَّارِ

Bismillahi-il-kabeer, A'oodhu billahi-il-azeemi-min-sharri-kulli-l'rqi'n-na'aarin, wa-min-sharri-harrin'naar.

"In the name of Allah, the Great, I seek refuge in Allah, the Magnificent, from the evil of bellowing veins, and from the evil of the Hellfire."

Source: Sunan Attermidhiy, Hadith No. 2075.

اللَّهُمَّ إِنِّي أَسْأَلُكَ بِأَنَّ لَكَ الْحَمْدَ، لاَ إِلَهَ إِلاَّ أَنْتَ الْحَنَّانُ بَدِيعَ السَّمَوَاتِ وَالأَرْضِ، يَا ذَا الْجَلالِ وَالإِكْرَامِ، يَا حَيُّ يَا قَيُّومُ

Allahumma innee As'aluka-bi-an'na-lakal-hamd, laa-ilaaha-anta, al-hunnaanu, badee'as-samaawaati-wal-ardh, ya zal-jalali-wa-l-ikraam, yaa hayyu-yaa qayyuum.

"O Allah, it is You Whom I beg for help, for to You all praise is due, and there is no god but You. You are the compassionate, the Originator of the Heavens and the earth, O You! the Lord of Majesty and Splendor. O You! the Living, the Eternal."

Source: Musnad Al-Imam Ahmad, Hadith No. 3/158.

اللَّهُمَّ إِنِّي أَسْأَلُكَ أَنِّي أَشْهَدُ أَنَّكَ أَنْتَ اللهُ الَّذِي لاَ إِلَهَ إِلاَّ أَنْتَ، الأَحَدُ، الصَّمَدُ، الَّذِي لَمْ يَلِدْ، وَلَمْ يُولَدْ، وَلَمْ يَكُنْ لَهُ كُفُوًا أَحَدٌ

Allahumma innee As'aluka-anni-ash-hadu-an'naka-ant-Allahil-lazi-laa-ilaahaa-illah-anta, al-ahad-ul-samadu-allazi-lam-ya-lid-wa-lam-yoo-lad-wa-lam-yakun-lahoo-kufuwan-ahad.

"O Allah, it is You Whom I beg for help, for I bear witness that there is no God but You, the One, the eternally besought of all, Who begets not, nor is He begotten; and to Whom none is comparable."

Source: Musnad Al-Imam Ahmad, Hadith No. 5/350. & Saheeh Ibn-Hibbaan, Hadith No. 891.

اللّهُمَّ عافِنِي في بَدَنِي ، اللّهُمَّ عافِنِي في سَمْعِي ، اللّهُمَّ عافِنِي في بَصَرِي ، لا إلهَ إلاّ أَنْتَ

Allahumma aafinee fee badanee, Allahumma aafinee fee samm'ee, Allahumma afinee fee basaree laa-ilaaha-illa-anta

"O Allah, make my body healthy, my hearing healthy and my eyesight healthy. There is no God but You."

Source: Sunan Abu-Daawuud, Hadith No. 5090. & Sunan Attermidhiy, Hadith No. 3480.

اللّهُمَّ اغْفِرْلِي وَارْحَمْنِي وَعَافِنِي وَاهْدِنِي وَارْزُقْنِي

Allahumma-ighfirli-war-hamni-wa-aafinee-wa-ahdinee-war-zuqni.

"O Allah, forgive my sins; have mercy on me; make me healthy; guide me; and provide for me."

Source: Musnad Al-Imam Ahmad, Hadith No. 4/353.

اللّهُمَّ بَرِّدْ قَلْبِي بِالثَّلْجِ وَالْبَرَدِ وَالْمَاءِ الْبَارِدِ اللّهُمَّ نَقِّ قَلْبِي مِنْ الْخَطَايَا كَمَا نَقَّيْتَ الثَّوْبَ الْأَبْيَضَ مِنْ الدَّنَسِ

Allahumma bar'rid-qalbee-bil-thaljee wal-bar'adi wa-l-maa'ai-l-baarid, Allahumma naqqi-qalbee-min-al-khatayya kama-naqaiyta-al-thowba-al-ab'yadaa-min-al-dan'nasi.

"O Allah! Cool my heart with ice, hail and cool water, and purify it of all sins, as a white garment is cleansed of all dirt."

Source: Sunan Attermidhiy, Hadith No. 3547.

اللّهُمَّ إِنِّي أَسْأَلُكَ العافِيةَ في الدُّنْيا وَالآخِرَة ، اللّهُمَّ إِنِّي أَسْأَلُكَ

العَفْوَ وَالعافِيةَ في ديني وَدُنْيايَ وَأَهْلي وَمالي ، اللّهُمَّ اسْتُرْ

عوْراتي وَآمِنْ رَوْعاتي ، اللّهُمَّ احْفَظْني مِن بَيْنِ يَدَيَّ وَمِن خَلْفي

وَعَن يَميني وَعَن شِمالي ، وَمِن فَوْقي ، وَأَعوذُ بِعَظَمَتِكَ أَن أُغْتالَ

مِن تَحْتي

Allahumma innee As'alukal-aafiyata fid-duniya-wal aakhirati, Allahumma innee as'alukal afwa wal aaffiyata fee deenee wa dunyaaya, wa-aahlee-wa-maalee, Allahum-mastur awratee, wa aa-min-rawaatee, Allahum-ma-ahfadhnee min-baiyni yaddayya wa-min-khalfee, wa-an yameenee, wa-an-shemaalee, wa-min-fawqee, wa-a'oodhu-bi-adhmatikaa un-ughtala min-tahtee.

"O Allah, I ask You for safety in this world and in the Hereafter. O Allah! I ask You for forgiveness and safety for soundness of my faith, and for my worldly affairs, my family and my property. O Allah! cover up my awraat, and keep me safe from the things I fear. O Allah! Guard me in front and back, right and left, and above; and I seek refuge in Your Greatness from unexpected harm from beneath."

Source: Sunan Abu-Daawuud, Hadith No. 5074.

اللهمَّ إِنِّي اعُوذُ بِرِضَاكَ مِنْ سَخَطِكَ و[أَعُوذُ] ، وَبِمُعَافَاتِكَ مِنْ عُقُوبتكَ ، وَأَعُوذُ بِكَ مِنْكَ لا أُحْصِي ثَنَاءً عَلَيْكَ ، أَنْتَ كَمَا أَثْنَيْتَ عَلَى نَفسِكَ

Allahumma innee A'oodhu bi-ridhaka -min -sakhitika,wa-a'oodhu-bi-mu'aafatika min uqoobatikaa, wa a'oodhubika minka, laa-uhsi' sanaa'aa alaiy'kaa, anta-kama-athnaiytaa alaa-nafsi'kaa.

"O Allah! I seek refuge in Your pleasure, from Your wrath, in Your pardon from Your punishment, and in You from You. Never can my praise of You be as much as Your praise of Yourself."

Source: Saheeh Muslim, Hadith No. 486. & Sunan Attermidhiy, Hadith No. 3566.

اللَّهُمَّ إِنِّي عَبْدُكَ وَابْنُ عَبْدِكَ وَابْنُ أَمَتِكَ نَاصِيَتِي بِيَدِكَ مَاضٍ فِيَّ حُكْمُكَ عَدْلٌ فِيَّ قَضَاؤُكَ أَسْأَلُكَ بِكُلِّ اسْمٍ هُوَ لَكَ سَمَّيْتَ بِهِ نَفْسَكَ أَوْ أَنْزَلْتَهُ فِي كِتَابِكَ أَوْ عَلَّمْتَهُ أَحَدًا مِنْ خَلْقِكَ أَوِ اسْتَأْثَرْتَ بِهِ فِي عِلْمِ الْغَيْبِ عِنْدَكَ أَنْ تَجْعَلَ الْقُرْآنَ رَبِيعَ قَلْبِي وَنُورَ صَدْرِي وَجِلَاءَ حُزْنِي وَذَهَابَ هَمِّي

Allahumma innee abduk (a) wa-bnu abdik (a), wa-bnu amatik (a), naaSiyaatee bi-yadik (a), maaDin fiyya ĥukmuk (a), adlun fiyya

115

qaDaa-uk, as'aluka bikullismin huwalak (a), sammayta bihi nafsak (a), aw-anzaltahu fee kitaabik (a), aw allamtahu ahadam-minkhalaqik (a), aw-ista'thart (a), bihi fee ilmil-ghaybi indak (a), antaja'l-alquraana rabeea qalbee, wa nuura SaDree, wa-jilaa'a huznee, wa dahaaba hammeel

"O Allah, I am Your slave, son of Your bondman and bondwoman. My forehead is in Your Hand. Your command concerning me prevails, and Your judgement of me is just. By each of Your names, with which You have described Yourself, which You have revealed in Your Book, which You may have taught to some of Your creatures, or which You have decided to keep unknown, I pray to You to make the Quran the delight of my heart, the light of my breast and the remover of my grief and distress."

Source: Musnad Al-Imam Ahmad, Hadith No. 1/391.

اللَّهُمَّ رَحْمَتَكَ أَرْجُو فَلَا تَكِلْنِي إِلَى نَفْسِي طَرْفَةَ عَيْنٍ، وَأَصْلِحْ لِي شَأْنِي كُلَّهُ لَا إِلَهَ إِلَّا أَنْتَ

Allahumma Rahmataka Arju fala takilni ila nafsee tarfat (a) ainin wa aslih li shaani kullahu laa –illaha- illaha anta (a)

"O Allah, it is Your mercy that I seek. I beg you not to abandon me to myself, even for as short a period as a wink. I beg You to set right all my affairs. There is no God but You."

Source: Sunan Abu-Daawuud, Hadith No. 5090.

يَا ذَا الْجَلَالِ وَالْإِكْرَامِ، يَا حَيُّ يَا قَيُّومُ ،بِرَحْمَتِكَ أَسْتَغِيثُ

Yaa daljalal-wal-ikram, ya hayyu yaa qayyum (u), birahmatika astagheeth

"O You Lord of Majesty and Splendor, O You the Living, the Self-subsistent; by Your Grace I seek help."

Source: Sunan Attermidhiy, Hadith No. 1525. & Musnad Al-Imam Ahmad, Hadith No. 3524.

اللَّهُ اللَّهُ رَبِّى؛ لاَ أُشْرِكُ بِهِ شَيْئاً

Allahu Allahu Rabbi, la ushriku bihi shaeea (a)

"Allah, Allah, He is my Lord. I do not associate anyone with Him."

Source: Sunan Abu-Daawuud, Hadith No. 1525, & Musnad Al-Imam Ahmad, Hadith No. 6/369.

حَسْبِيَ اللّهُ لا إِلهَ إِلاّ هُوَ عَلَيهِ تَوَكَّلتُ وَهُوَ رَبُّ العَرْشِ العَظِيم

Hasbiya- Allahu laa illaha illa huwa alaihi tawakaltu wa-huwa rabbul arshil-azeem

"Allah suffices me. There is no God but He. In Him is my trust, and He is Lord of the Glorious Throne."

Source: Sunan Abu-Daawuud, Hadith No. 5081.

لاَ بَأْسَ عَلَيْكَ طَهُورٌ، إِنْ شَاءَ

La-baasa alaika, tahoorun inn-shaa-Allah

"May your suffering end. May you be purified by Allah's Grace."

Source: Saheeh Al-Bukhari, Hadith No. 5656.

اللَّهُمَّ آتِ نَفْسِي تَقْوَاهَا، وَزَكِّهَا أَنْتَ خَيْرُ مَنْ زَكَّاهَا، أَنْتَ وَلِيُّهَا وَمَوْلَاهَا، اللَّهُمَّ إِنِّي أَعُوذُ بِكَ مِنْ عِلْمٍ لَا يَنْفَعُ، وَمِنْ قَلْبٍ لَا يَخْشَعُ، وَمِنْ نَفْسٍ لَا تَشْبَعُ، وَمِنْ دَعْوَةٍ لَا يُسْتَجَابُ لَهَا

Allahumma-aa'ti nafsee-taqwaaha, wa, zakkiha-anta-khaiyroo-man-zakkahaa, anta waleeyoo'haa wa-mawlaahaa, Allahumma innee a'oodhubika min-ilm-il-la yanfaa'oo, wa-min-qalbin-la-yakhsha'oo, wa-min-nafsin la-tashbaa'oo, wa-min-da'watin la-yustajaabaa-lahaa.

"O Allah, I beg You to grant my soul its proper taqwa, and to refine it. You are the best in refining. You are its helper and master. O Allah, I seek refuge in You from knowledge that is not beneficial, a heart that is not submissive, a soul that is not contented, and a supplication that is not answerable."

Source: Saheeh Muslim # 2722

اللَّهُمَّ صَلِّ عَلَى مُحَمَّدٍ وَعَلَى آلِ مُحَمَّدٍ كَمَا صَلَّيْتَ عَلَى إِبْرَاهِيمَ وَعَلَى آلِ إِبْرَاهِيمَ. إِنَّكَ حَمِيدٌ مَجِيدٌ اللَّهُمَّ بَارِكْ عَلَى مُحَمَّدٍ،

وَعَلَى آلِ مُحَمَّدٍ كَمَا بَارَكْتَ عَلَى إِبْرَاهِيمَ وَعَلَى آلِ إِبْرَاهِيمَ . إِنَّكَ حَمِيدٌ مَجِيدٌ

Allahumma Salli Alla Muhammadiwo Wa Alla-Aale-Muhammadin Kamaa Sallaita Ala Ibraahima Wa-Alla Aale Ibraahima Inn'naka-Hammeedum-Majeed. Allahumma Baarik Alla Muhammadiwo Wa-Ala Aale Muhammadin Kama Baarakta Ala Ibraahima-Wa-Alla Aale Ibraahima Inn'naka –hammedum-Majeed

"O Allah, pray for Muhammad and the family of Muhammad, as You have prayed for Ibraheem and the family of Ibraheem. You are praiseworthy and gloryworthy. O Allah! Bless Muhammad and the family of Muhammad, as You have blessed Ibraheem and the family of Ibraheem, in all the worlds. You are praiseworthy and gloryworthy."

Source: Saheeh Al-Bukhari, Hadith No. 3370. & Saheeh Muslim, Hadith No. 406.

13.4 Comprehensive Quranic Ruqyah Treatment

The verses in this section are those that scholars have used to treat severe cases of sihr and other related ailments. [Source: "Self Ruqyah Treatment" by Dr. K. Al-Jeraisy].

1. Surah Al-Faatiha
2. Surah Al-Baqarah (Verses 1 – 7)
3. Surah Al-Baqarah (Verses 117)
4. Surah Al-Baqarah (Verses 137)
5. Surah Al-Baqarah (Verses 163 – 164)
6. Surah Al-Baqarah (Verses 254 – 257)
7. Surah Al-Baqarah (Verses 284 – 286)
8. Surah # 3 (Verses 1 – 6)

9. Surah # 3 (Verses 18)
10. Surah # 3 (Verses 26 – 27)
11. Surah # 3 (Verses 85)
12. Surah # 7 (Verses 54 – 56)
13. Surah # 21 (Verses 87)
14. Surah # 17 (Verses 110 – 111)
15. Surah # 2 (Verse 109)
16. Surah # 4 (Verse 54)
17. Surah # 10 (Verse 107)
18. Surah # 12 (Verse 67)
19. Surah # 18 (Verse 39)
20. Surah # 67 (Verse 1 – 4)
21. Surah # 68 (Verse 51 – 52)
22. Surah # 2 (Verse 102 – 103)
23. Surah # 7 (Verse 117 – 122)
24. Surah # 10 (Verse 77)
25. Surah # 10 (Verse 81 – 82)
26. Surah # 20 (Verse 69)
27. Surah # 23 (Verse 115 – 118)
28. Surah # 46 (Verse 31)
29. Surah # 55 (Verse 33 – 36)
30. Surah # 59 (Verse 21 – 24)
31. Surah # 6 (Verse 17)
32. Surah # 37 (Verse 1 – 11)
33. Surah # 6 (Verse 13)
34. Surah # 9 (Verse 129)
35. Surah # 39 (Verse 38)
36. Surah # 65 (Verse 7)
37. Surah # 10 (Verse 62 – 63)
38. Surah # 12 (Verse 86)
39. Surah # 13 (Verse 28)
40. Surah # 14 (Verse 27)
41. Surah # 35 (Verse 34)
42. Surah # 94 (Verse 1 – 8)
43. Surah # 41 (Verse 44)
44. Surah # 10 (Verse 57)
45. Surah # 17 (Verse 82)

46. Surah # 9 (Verse 14 – 15)
47. Surah # 17 (Verse 81)
48. Surah # 23 (Verse 107)
49. Surah # 2 (Verse 72)
50. Surah # 25 (Verse 23)
51. Surah # 65 (Verse 2 – 3)
52. Surah # 87 (Verse 4)
53. Surah # 99
54. Surah # 12 (Verse 64)
55. Surah # 15 (Verse 17)
56. Surah # 40 (Verse 44 – 45)
57. Surah # 82 (Verse 10 – 12)
58. Surah # 86 (Verse 4)
59. Surah Al-Kafiroon
60. Surah Al-Ikhlas
61. Al-Mi'wadhatayn (Surah Al-Falaq and Surah An-Naass)

According to a hadith that is attributed to the prophet (s.a.w.), he recited the following verses as a ruqyah. (Musnad Abi Yaala Al-Moosli, Hadith # 1583).

- Surah Al-Faatihah
- Surah Al-Baqarah verses 1 – 4
- Surah Al-Baqarah verses 163 – 164
- Surah Al-Baqarah verse 255 (Ayat-ul-Kursi)
- Surah Al-Baqarah verses (284 – 286)
- Surah Aal-e-Imran verse 18
- Surah Al-Aaraaf verse 54
- Surah Al-Mu'minoon verse 116
- Surah jinn Verse 3
- Surah As-Saffaat verse 1 – 10
- Surah Al-Hashr verse 22 – 24
- Surah Ikhlas
- Al- Mu'wadaitain

14 Considerations in Removal of Sihr

This chapter covers some of the key considerations for the removal of black magic as prescribed in the Quran and Sunnah.

Reciting Ruqyah over Water / Oil

One method recommended by scholars is to recite Quranic ruqyah over enough water for taking a bath and then pouring that water over one's body. The scholars have also mentioned that one may recite Quran into water, some of which should be taken by the person who has been affected by sihr, and he should wash with the rest one or more times as needed. This will remove the sihr by Allah's Leave. This was mentioned by many scholars including Shaykh Abd Al-Rahmaan ibn Hasan in Fath Al-Majeed Sharh Kitaab Al-Tawheed, in (the chapter entitled) "Baab Ma jaaA fi'l-Nushrah", and by others.

It is also stated that along with reciting ruqyah over water, one can recite Quranic verses on oil and apply that oil on the body (Musnad Ahmad 497/3 # 16055, and authenticated by Albani in his Ahadith series 108/1 # 379).

Using Lotus (Sidr) Leaves in Ruqyah Treatment

Another remedy recommended by scholars calls for mixing ground lotus leaves in clean water and then reciting Quranic ruqyah over the mixture and then using that water (by pouring) as mentioned earlier. This was mentioned by many scholars including Shaykh Abd Al-Rahmaan ibn Hasan in Fath Al-Majeed Sharh Kitaab Al-Tawheed, in (the chapter entitled) "Baab Ma jaaA fi'l-Nushrah", and by others. This is also mentioned by Sheikh Munajjid in islamqa.info.)

Removal of Objects Used for Sihr

One of the considerations in the treatment of sihr is to find and remove any objects that were used in casting sihr or black magic on others. This obviously can be done only when these objects are known. For example, some people may find strange objects buried in their backyards or other places that they may suspect have been used in casting black magic upon them. This is known to be a common tactic used by magicians and the hadith states that this was also done by a man named *Labid Ben Al-Aasam* who performed sihr on the prophet (s.a.w.).

It is mentioned in Tafsir Ibn Kathir that In the Book of Medicine of his Saheeh, Al-Bukhari recorded that A'ishah said, *"The Messenger of Allah was bewitched until he thought that he had relations with his wives, but he had not had relations with them."* Sufyan said, "This is the worst form of magic when it reaches this stage." So the prophet (s.a.w.) said,

«يَا عَائِشَةُ، أَعَلِمْتِ أَنَّ اللهَ قَدْ أَفْتَانِي فِيمَا اسْتَفْتَيْتُهُ فِيهِ؟ أَتَانِي رَجُلَانِ فَقَعَدَ أَحَدُهُمَا عِنْدَ رَأْسِي وَالْآخَرُ عِنْدَ رِجْلَيَّ، فَقَالَ الَّذِي عِنْدَ رَأْسِي لِلْآخَرِ: مَا بَالُ الرَّجُلِ؟ قَالَ: مَطْبُوبٌ، قَالَ: وَمَنْ طَبَّهُ، قَالَ: لَبِيدُ بْنُ أَعْصَمَ: رَجُلٌ مِنْ بَنِي زُرَيْقٍ حَلِيفٌ لِيَهُودَ، كَانَ مُنَافِقًا، قَالَ: وَفِيمَ؟ قَالَ: فِي مُشْطٍ وَمُشَاطَةٍ، قَالَ: وَأَيْنَ؟ قَالَ: فِي جُفِّ طَلْعَةِ ذَكَرٍ، تَحْتَ رَاعُوفَةٍ فِي بِئْرِ ذَرْوَانَ»

"(O `A'ishah! Do you know that Allah has answered me concerning that which I asked Him? Two men came to me and one of them sat by my head while the other sat by my feet. The one who was sitting by my head said to the other one, `What is wrong with this man?' The other replied, `He is bewitched.' The first one said, `Who bewitched him?' The other replied, `Labid bin Asam. He is a man from the tribe of Banu Zurayq who is an ally of the Jews, and a hypocrite.' The first one asked, `With what did he bewitch him?' The other replied, `With a comb and hair from the comb.' The first one asked, `Where is the comb?' The other answered, `In the dried bark of a male date palm under a rock in a well called Dharwan.') `A'ishah said, "So he went to the well to remove it (the comb with the hair)?" Then he said,

$$\text{«هَذِهِ الْبِئْرُ الَّتِي أُرِيتُهَا، وَكَأَنَّ مَاءَهَا نُقَاعَةُ الحِنَّاءِ،وَكَأَنَّ نَخْلَهَا رُؤُوسُ الشَّيَاطِينِ»}$$

"This is the well that I saw. It was as if its water had henna soaked in it and its palm trees were like the heads of devils.) So he removed it (of the well). Then I (`A'ishah) said, 'Will you not make this public?'" He replied,

$$\text{«أَمَّا اللهُ فَقَدْ شَفَانِي، وَأَكْرَهُ أَنْ أُثِيرَ عَلَى أَحَدٍ مِنَ النَّاسِ شَرًّا»}$$

"Allah has cured me and I hate to spread (the news of) wickedness to any of the people.)"

Preventing Sihr

As "prevention is better than cure," a Muslim should take appropriate measures to prevent oneself from the attacks of sihr in case if some evil decides to cast it. The following are some of the measures that one can take as stipulated in both the Quran and Sunnah. These were also mentioned earlier in the book and are summarized again below.

124

- Recite Aayat Al-Kursiy [Surah Al-Baqarah, 2:255] after every prescribed prayer (after finishing the adhkaar (Allah's remembrances), which are prescribed at the end of the obligatory prayers).
- Recite Aayat Al-Kursiy when going to sleep. This is in line with the guidance of the prophet (s.a.w.) who said in a saheeh report: *"Whoever recites Aayat Al-Kursiy at night will have ongoing protection from Allah and no devil will come near him until morning comes."*
- Recite surah Al-Ikhlas, surah An-Nas and surah Al-Falaq after every obligatory prayer.
- Recite Surah Al-Ikhlas and al-Muwadtain at the beginning of the day after Fajr prayers, and at the beginning of the evening after Maghrib prayers.
- Recite the last two verses of surah Al-Baqarah each evening. According to a hadith, the prophet (s.a.w.) said: "Whoever recites the last two verses of surah Al-Baqarah at night, it will suffice him."
- Seek refuge in the words of Allah, from all the evil which He has created, constantly and at all times. The prophet (s.a.w.) said: *"Whoever stops to rest and says, A'oodhu bi kalimaat Allah il-taammah min sharri ma khalaq (I seek refuge in the perfect words of Allah from the evil of that which He has created),' nothing will harm him until he moves on from that place."*
- Say the dua "Bismillaah alladhi laa yadurr maA ismihi shay'un fi'l-ardi wa laa fi'l-samaa'i wa huwa Al-samee' Al-Aleem (In the name of Allah with Whose name nothing on earth or in heaven can cause harm, and He is the All-Hearing, All-Knowing)" at the beginning of the day and the beginning of the night (three times). According to saheeh reports, the prophet (s.a.w.) urged us to recite this, and this is a means of keeping safe from all evil.
- Eat 7 Ajwah dates in the morning as the prophet (s.a.w.) instructed us to do. The hadith states the following:

مَنْ اصْطَبَحَ بِسَبْعِ تَمَرَاتٍ عَجْوَةً لَمْ يَضُرَّهُ ذَلِكَ الْيَوْمِ سُمٌّ "
"وَلَا سِحْرٌ

"Whoever starts his morning by taking seven Ajwa dates, he will not be harmed by poisoning or sihr (witchcraft)"

Al-Bukhari MaAl Fatah, 247/10, # 5445, Muslim 1618/3 # 2047.

Blessings of Zamzam water

Zamzam water has enormous blessings and cures as was told to us by the prophet (s.a.w.). He (s.a.w.) said concerning the water of Zamzam,

"It is a blessing, and it is food that satisfies." (Reported by Muslim, 4/1922).

Al-Abbaas ibn Abd al-Muttalib said: *"The people used to compete over Zamzam during the time of Jaahiliyyah. People who had children used to bring them and give them to drink."* Al-'Abbaas said: *"During the Jaahiliyyah, Zamzam was known as Shabaa'ah (satisfaction)."*

The prophet (s.a.w.) said:

"The water of Zamzam is for whatever purpose it is drunk for." (Reported by Ibn Maajah, 2/1018; see Al-Maqaasid al-Hasanah by al-Sakhaawi, p. 359).

Ibn al-Mubaarak entered Zamzam and said, *"O Allah, Ibn al-Muammal told me, from Abul-Zubayr from Jaabir that the Messenger of Allah (s.a.w.) said: 'The water of Zamzam is for whatever purpose it is drunk for,' so, O Allah, I am drinking it (to quench) my thirst on the Day of Resurrection."*

We know from a well known hadith that during the times when the prophet (s) was bestowed with revelations from Allah, his chest was washed by the angels withZamzam water. The Prophet (s.a.w.) said:

> *"My roof was opened when I was in Makkah, and Jibreel (peace be upon him) came down and opened my chest, then he washed it with Zamzam water. Then he brought a gold basin full of wisdom and faith, poured it into my chest, and closed it up again. Then he took me by the hand and ascended with me into the first heaven." (Reported by al-Bukhaari, 3/429).*

Al-Haafiz al-'Iraaqi (may Allah have mercy on him) said: *"The reason why the Prophet's chest was washed with Zamzam water was to make him stronger so that he could see the kingdom of heaven and earth, and Paradise and Hell, because one of the special qualities of Zamzam is that it strengthens the heart and calms the soul."*

It is sunnah to drink one's fill of Zamzam water and to quench one's thirst.

It was reported that when Ibn 'Abbaas (may Allah be pleased with him) drank from the water of Zamzam, he said: *"O Allah, I ask you for beneficial knowledge, plentiful provision and healing from every disease."*

Some fuqaha' recommended that people should take some Zamzam water back with them to their countries, because it is a cure for those who seek healing. Aa'ishah reported that she took Zamzam water home with her in bottles, and said, "The Messenger of Allah (s.a.w.) took some of it away with him, and he used to pour it on the sick and give it to them to drink." (Reported by al-Tirmidhi, 4/37). She also reported the following about the prophet (s.a.w.):

> *"...he used to carry it in small vessels and buckets, and pour it onto the sick and give it to them to drink. Whenever a guest visited Ibn 'Abbaas he would honor him by giving him Zamzam*

to drink. 'Ata' was asked about taking Zamzam water away, and he said: "The Prophet (s.a.w.), al-Hasan and al-Husayn all took it away with them." [Source: Tirmidhi 180/1 #963, wa albehaqi 202/5, Authenticated by Albani in Sahih Tirmidhi 284/1, and silsilah alahadith alsahih 572/2 #883, and Zaad al MaAd392/4.]

Ibn Al-Qayyim mentions in Zaad Al-Maad:

وَقَدْ جَرَّبْتُ أَنَا وَغَيْرِي مِنَ الِاسْتِشْفَاءِ بِمَاءِ زَمْزَمَ أُمُورًا عَجِيبَةً،

وَاسْتَشْفَيْتُ بِهِ مِنْ عِدَّةِ أَمْرَاضٍ،

"…And I and others experimented healing through Zamzam water and and observed amazing matters and got healed from a number of diseases…" [Zaad al MaAd 393/4]

Blessings of Olive Oil

The olive tree is mentioned in the Quran for its purity and blessings. Scholars, therefore, recommend that Quranic ruqyah can be recited over olive oil, which then is used by the patient in various ways such applying on the skin and hair and even as a food.

Allah says in the Quran:

اللَّهُ نُورُ السَّمَاوَاتِ وَالْأَرْضِ ۚ مَثَلُ نُورِهِ كَمِشْكَاةٍ فِيهَا مِصْبَاحٌ ۖ الْمِصْبَاحُ فِي زُجَاجَةٍ ۖ الزُّجَاجَةُ كَأَنَّهَا كَوْكَبٌ دُرِّيٌّ يُوقَدُ مِن شَجَرَةٍ مُّبَارَكَةٍ زَيْتُونَةٍ لَّا شَرْقِيَّةٍ وَلَا غَرْبِيَّةٍ يَكَادُ زَيْتُهَا يُضِيءُ وَلَوْ لَمْ

تَمْسَسْهُ نَارٌ ۚ نُورٌ عَلَىٰ نُورٍ ۗ يَهْدِي اللَّهُ لِنُورِهِ مَن يَشَاءُ ۚ
وَيَضْرِبُ اللَّهُ الْأَمْثَالَ لِلنَّاسِ ۗ وَاللَّهُ بِكُلِّ شَيْءٍ عَلِيمٌ ﴾

"Allah is the Light of the heavens and the earth. The parable of His Light is as (if there were) a niche and within it a lamp, the lamp is in glass, the glass as it were a brilliant star, lit from a blessed tree, an olive, neither of the east (i.e., it neither gets sun-rays only in the morning) nor of the west (i.e., nor does it get sun-rays only in the afternoon – but it is exposed to the sun all day long), whose oil would almost glow forth (of itself), though no fire touched it. Light upon Light! Allah guides to His Light whom He wills. And Allah sets forth parables for mankind, and Allah is All-Knower of everything." [Surah al-Noor, 24:35]

In surah Al-Mu'minoon, Allah says:

﴿وَشَجَرَةً تَخْرُجُ مِن طُورِ سَيْنَاءَ تَنبُتُ بِالدُّهْنِ وَصِبْغٍ لِّلْآكِلِينَ﴾

"And a tree (olive) that springs forth from Mount Sinai, that grows oil, and (it is a) relish for the eaters." [Surah al-Mu'minoon, 23:20]

Abu Aseed said: "The Prophet (s.a.w.) said: "Eat the oil and use it on your hair and skin, for it comes from a blessed tree." (Reported by al-Tirmidhi, 1775; see also Saheeh al-Jaami')

15 Considerations in Treating Evil Eye

As mentioned earlier, a person can easily be affected by the evil eye of enviers and those who are jealous. The scholars have stated that with regard to dealing with the evil eye and hasad (destructive envy), there is no doubt that when a person is close to Allah, always remembering Him (dhikr) and reading the Quran, he is less likely to be affected by the evil eye and other kinds of harm from the evils of mankind and the jinn. The following are steps from the Quran and hadith that the scholars have prescribed for the treatment of evil eye.

Recitation of Muwadaitain and Surah Ikhlas

The most common treatment for evil eye is to recite the *Muwadaitain* regularly. We know from Abi Saeed Al-Khudri that the prophet (s.a.w.) used to seek Allah's protection from the evil eye of humans and the jinn but after the Muwadaitain were revelaed he started reciting these Surahs and left the others (Nisaee # 544).

In a hadeeth narrated by Al-Bukhaari in his Saheeh which was attributed to Aa'ishah (may Allah be pleased with her) she said: *"When the prophet (s.a.w.) went to bed each night, he would put his hands together and blow in between them and recite in between them: Qul huwa Allahu ahad (Say: He is Allah, (the) One), Qul a'oodhu bi Rabbi'l-Falaq (Say: I seek refuge with (Allah) the Lord of the daybreak) and Qul a'oodhu bi Rabbi'n-naas (Say: I seek refuge with (Allah) the Lord of mankind) [i.e., the last three surahs of the Quran], then he would wipe with his hands whatever he could of his body, starting with his head and face, and the front part of his body, doing that three times."*

Reciting the Duas for the Evil Eye

In al-Saheehayn, it is narrated that Aaishah said: *"The prophet (s.a.w.) commanded me or he commanded us to recite ruqyah for protection against the evil eye."* We find a number of Duas from the hadith that scholars have recommended for protection from evil eye. Among them are the following:

We learn from ahadith that angel Jibreel taught the prophet (s.a.w.) Dua for illnesses too. Abu Sa'eed reports that Jibreel came to the prophet (s.a.w.) and said: "O Muhammad, are you ill?" He said, "Yes." He said,

بِسْمِ الله أَرْقِيكَ، مِنْ كُلِّ شَيْءٍ يُؤْذِيكَ، وَمِنْ شَرِّ كُلِّ نَفْسٍ أَوْ عَيْنٍ حَاسِدٍ، اللهُ يَشْفِيكَ، بِسمِ اللهِ أَرقِيكَ

"Bismillaah arqeeka min kulli shay'in yu'dheeka, wa min sharri kulli nafsin aw Aynin haasid Allah yashfeek, bismillaah arqeek

"In the name of Allah I perform ruqyah for you, from everything that is harming you, from the evil of every soul or envious eye, may Allah heal you, in the name of Allah I perform ruqyah for you" [Source: Saheeh Muslim as narrated by Abu Sayeed 1718/4 #2186].

This dua and others related to the evil eye mentioned in chapter 13 should be recited three times or more.

Washing

If the person who casts an evil eye is known or suspected, then in line with the traditions of the prophet (s.a.w.) the scholars have recommended that that person (who cast the evil eye) should be ordered to wash himself in a vessel. Then the water should be poured over the head of the one on whom he cast the evil eye, pouring it from behind in one go. Then he will be healed by Allah's leave. This is because the prophet (s.a.w.) commanded Aamir ibn Rabeeah to do so in a hadeeth quoted earlier in chapter 6.

[Sources: (a) Al-Tirmidhi, 2060; Abu Dawood, 4737. And he would say, "Thus Ibraaheem used to seek refuge with Allah for Ishaaq and Ismaa'eel, peace be upon them both" (narrated by Al-Bukhaari, 3371). (b) Fataawa Al-Shaykh Ibn Uthaymeen, 2/117, 118. (c) Fataawa Al-Lajnah Al-Daa'imah li'l-Buhooth Al-'Ilmiyyah wa'l-Ifta, 1/186.)

Preventive Steps to Ward Off Evil Eye

The following are some of the steps that one can take to prevent evil eye from hurting oneself:

- Scholars have stated that women should cover their beauty by following Islamic guidelines of covering oneself. This will minimize being affected by evil eye (islamqa.info).
- One should seek refuge with Allah by regularly reciting Quran, and specifically the Mi'wadhatayn (the last two Surahs of the Quran, Al-Falaq and Al-Naas), Surah Al-Faatihah and Aayat Al-Kursiy [Al-Baqarah, 2:255].
- The following two duas should be recited by the person who fears that his eye is envious (Zaad al Maa'd).

When seeing something that the person likes, he should say the following:

"Allahumma, Barik 'Alaihi"

"Oh, Allah! Bless him," as the Messenger of Allah commanded 'Amir to say to Sahl. And among the things which alleviate it is the saying:

"Ma Sha'allahu La Quwwata Illa Billah"

"That which Allah wills (will come to pass).There is no strength except with Allah."

Whenever 'Urwah saw something he admired, or he entered any of his gardens, he would say this.

- Regularly reciting from the duas mentioned earlier and to constantly seek refuge from Shaytaan. The prophet (s.a.w.) used to seek refuge for Al-Hasan and Al-Husayn and say:

   U'eedhukuma bi kalimaat Allah Al-taammati min kulli Shaytanin wa haammah wa min kulli Aynin laammah

(I seek refuge for you both in the perfect words of Allah, from every devil and every poisonous reptile, and from every evil eye).

16 Jinn Possession Treatment

Similar to other ailments, jinn possession can be cured only through the Quran and its recitation. As mentioned earlier, the ailment of jinn possession is real as mentioned in the Quran, surah Al-Baqarah, and verse 275. The Quranic ruqyah mentioned in chapter 13 can also be used to rid one of jinn possession.

When seeking treatment for jinn possession, it is important to seek the advice of learned scholars. It is important to note that the only treatment of jinn possession is through the Quran and dua from Quran and hadith. Anyone who claims to treat jinn possession through any other means may be committing acts of shirk.

Any words used that are not from the Quran or sunnah and words whose meanings are not understood constitute as *shirk*. Some magicians use Jinns and satanic verses to invoke Satan and Jinns and all such words and actions – no matter how effective they may seem – are completely against the teachings of Islam because they involve treatment using entities other than Allah. The scholars of hadith have clearly stated that such tactics are haram and are meant to fool people and to get money. The only authorized treatment is by reciting the Quran and dua [Source: Majmoo' Fataawa al-Shaykh Saalih al-Fawzan (1/52)].

Shaykh Abd Al-Azeez ibn Abd-Allah ibn Baaz (may Allah have mercy on him) stated the following about seeking treatment of sihr through the use of Jinn:

> *The sick person should not use the services of the jinn for treatment or ask them for anything, rather he should ask well known doctors (scholars), but he should not turn to the jinn, because that is a means that leads to*

worshipping them and believing them. Among the jinn are some who are kaafirs and some who are Muslims, and some who are innovators, and you do not know about them. So you should not rely on them or ask them for anything, even if they appear to you. Rather you should ask the people of knowledge and human doctors. Allah condemned the mushrikeen as He said:

"And verily, there were men among mankind who took shelter with the males among the jinn, but they (Jinn) increased them (mankind) in sin and transgression" [Surah Al-Jinn, 72:6].

And it is a means that leads to dependence upon them and shirk, and it leads to seeking benefit from them and seeking their help, and all of that is shirk" [Source: Majallat Al-Da'wah (no. 1602, Rabee' Al-Awwal 1418AH, p. 34)].

When reciting Quran verses on a person who is affected or possessed by such an ailment, the reciter usually recites the Quran in the ear of the patient. Scholars have stated that reciting the Quran close to the ear of the patient causes the jinn (Shaytan) to run away [Source: Fatah al haq al Mubeen Fi I'laaj al SaraA wa ala'in, P-112, wa Bukhari #574].

17 Seeking Protection from Shaytan

As discussed in the previous chapters, most of the harm related to sihr and evil eye can be attributed to Shaytan. Our efforts, therefore, should be to keep Shaytan out of our homes and lives. We can protect ourselves from him by ensuring to remember Allah as that is a great means of protection from Shaytan. One of the salaf said: "*When dhikr becomes well-established in the heart, if the Shaytan gets too close, a person can defeat him. Then the shayateen gather around him (the Shaytan who tried to get close to the heart of the believer) and say, 'What is wrong with this one?' and it is said, 'He was harmed by a human!'*" (Madaarij al-Saalikeen, 2/424).

This chapter includes a few duas from the Quran and hadith that one can use to ward off Shaytan's effects from our lives. Ideally, these duas should be recited daily to prevent harm.

Reciting Mu'wadaitain

Reciting the last two Surahs from the Quran is one of the best deterrents against Shaytan. For example, in surah An-Naas Allah tells us to seek refuge from Shaytan, about whom Allah said:

$$﴿مِن شَرِّ الْوَسْوَاسِ الْخَنَّاسِ﴾$$

"(I seek protection) From the evil of the whisperer (devil who whispers evil in the hearts of men) who withdraws (from his whispering in one's heart after one remembers Allah)."

Ibn Kathir reports in his tafsir that Saeed bin Jubayr reported what Ibn Abbas said concerning Allah's statement in surah An-Naas:

"The devil is squatting (perched) upon the heart of the son of Adam. So when man becomes absent minded and heedless, Satan whispers to him. But, when he remembers Allah Satan withdraws."

Al-Mu`tamir bin Sulayman reported that his father said, "It has been mentioned to me that Shaytan is Al-Waswas. He blows into the heart of the son of Adam when he is sad and when he is happy. But when he (man) remembers Allah, Shaytan withdraws" (Al-Awfi reported from Ibn `Abbas).

The Blessings of Adhaan

It was narrated that Suhayl ibn Abi Saalih said: "My father sent me to Bani Haarithah, and I was with my companion. Someone called out his name from a garden, and the one who was with me looked into the garden and did not see anything. I mentioned that to my father, and he said, 'If I had known that this was going to happen to you, I would not have sent you. But if you hear such a voice then make the call for prayer, for I heard Abu Hurayrah (may Allah be pleased with him) narrating that the prophet (s.a.w.) said: "When the Shaytan hears the call to prayer, he runs away fast" (narrated by Muslim, 389).

Duas for Seeking Protection from Shaytan

The following duas can help one in seeking protection from Shaytaan.

اللَّهُمَّ إِنِّي أَعُوذُ بِكَ مِنَ الْهَدْمِ، وَأَعُوذُ بِكَ مِنَ التَّرَدِّي، وَأَعُوذُ بِكَ مِنَ الْغَرَقِ، وَالْحَرَقِ، وَالْهَرَمِ، وَأَعُوذُ بِكَ مِنْ أَنْ يَتَخَبَّطَنِيَ الشَّيْطَانُ عِنْدَ الْمَوْتِ.

Allahumma innee auuđu bika minal-hadm (i), wa auuđu bika minat-taraddi, wa auuđu bika minal-gharaq (i), wal-harq (i), wal-haram (i), wa auuđu bika min ay-yatakhabbaTaniyash-Shaytanu indal-mawt

"O Allah! I seek refuge in You from demolitions. I seek refuge in You from falling down from high places. I seek refuge in You from drowning, burning and old age. I seek refuge in You from Satan's temptations at death."

Source: Sunan Abu-Daawuud # 1552

أَعُوذُ بِكَلِمَاتِ اللَّهِ التَّامَّاتِ الَّتِي لَا يُجَاوِزُهُنَّ بَرٌّ وَلَا فَاجِرٌ، مِنْ شَرِّ مَا خَلَقَ، وَبَرَأَ، وَذَرَأَ، وَمِنْ شَرِّ مَا يَنْزِلُ مِنَ السَّمَاءِ، وَمِنْ شَرِّ مَا يَعْرُجُ فِيهَا، وَمِنْ شَرِّ مَا ذَرَأَ فِي الْأَرْضِ، وَمِنْ شَرِّ مَا يَخْرُجُ مِنْهَا، وَمِنْ شَرِّ فِتَنِ اللَّيْلِ وَالنَّهَارِ، وَمِنْ شَرِّ كُلِّ طَارِقٍ إِلَّا طَارِقًا يَطْرُقُ بِخَيْرٍ يَا رَحْمَنُ

Auuđu bi-wajhil-laahil-kareem (i), wa bi- kalimaatil-laahit-taamaat(i), allaatee laa yujaawizhunna barrow-walaa faajir (um), min-sharri maayanzilu minas-samaa'(i), wa sharri maa yaζruju feehaa, wa sharri maađara'a fil-arD(i) wa sharri maa yakhruju minhaa, wa min fitnatil-layliwan-nahaar(i), wa min Tawariqil-layliwan-nahaar(i), illaa TaariqayyaTruku bi-khayr(iy) yaa Rahmaan

"I seek refuge in Allah by Allah's Perfect Face and by His Perfect Words, which cannot be surpassed by the righteous or the profligate, from the evil of whatever comes down from heaven and whatever goes up to it, from the evil of whatever goes into the earth and whatever comes out of it, from the trials of night and day and from the knocking disasters of night and day, except a knocker bearing good. O You, the Merciful."

Source: Musnad Ahmad # 3/419

اللَّهُمَّ رَبَّ السَّمَاوَاتِ وَرَبَّ الأَرْضِ وَرَبَّ الْعَرْشِ الْعَظِيمِ، رَبَّنَا وَرَبَّ

كُلِّ شَيْءٍ، فَالِقَ الْحَبِّ وَالنَّوَى، وَمُنْزِلَ التَّوْرَاةِ وَالإِنْجِيلِ وَالْفُرْقَانِ،

أَعُوذُ بِكَ مِنْ شَرِّ كُلِّ شَيْءٍ أَنْتَ آخِذٌ بِنَاصِيَتِه، اللَّهُمَّ أَنْتَ الأَوَّلُ

فَلَيْسَ قَبْلَكَ شَيْءٌ، وَأَنْتَ الآخِرُ فَلَيْسَ بَعْدَكَ شَيْءٌ، وَأَنْتَ الظَّاهِرُ

فَلَيْسَ فَوْقَكَ شَيْءٌ، وَأَنْتَ الْبَاطِنُ فَلَيْسَ دُونَكَ شَيْءٌ، اقْضِ عَنَّا

الدَّيْنَ وَأَغْنِنَا مِنَ الْفَقْرِ

Allahumma rabbas-samaawaati wa-rabbal-arD (i), wa-rabbal-Arshil-AŽeem, rabbanaa wa-rabba kulli shay-in, faaliqal-ĥabbi wan-nawaa, wa-munzilat-tawraati wal-injeeli wal-furqaan, a'uuđu bika min sharri kulli shay-in anta aakhiđum-binaaSiyatih. Allahumma antal-awwal (u) fa-laysa qablaka shay-un, wa- antal-aakhir (u) fa-laysa ba'daka shay-un, wa- antaŽ-Žaahir(u) fa-laysa fawaqaka shay-a, wa- antal-baaTinu fa-laysa dunnaka shay-un, iqDi annad-dayn (a), wa-ghinna minal-faqr

"O Allah, Lord of the seven heavens and earth and the Magnificent Throne, our Lord and Lord of all things, the splitter and grower of the seed grain and date stone! The revealer of At-Tawraah, Al Injeel, and the Quran, I seek refuge in You from the evil of all things, which you hold under Your control. You are the first, nothing before You.

You are the Last, nothing after You. You are the manifest, nothing above You. You are the innermost, nothing beyond You. Remove the burden of our debt, and relieve us from poverty."

Source: Saheeh Muslim # 2713

It was narrated from Sulaymaan ibn Sard that two men were trading insults in the presence of the prophet (s.a.w.), until the face of one of them turned red. The prophet (s.a.w.) said, *"I know a word which, if he were to say it, will make what he is suffering from go away:*

A'oodhu Billaahi minash-Shaytanir-rajeem

"I seek refuge with Allah from the accursed Shaytan."

Source: al-Bukhaari, 3108; Muslim, 2610.

Abu Hurayrah reports that the Messenger of Allah (s.a.w.) said: *"Whoever says the following one hundred times in the day, will have a reward equivalent to that of freeing ten slaves, one hundred hasanahs (good deeds) will be recorded for him, and one hundred sayiAhs (bad deeds) will be erased from his record, and it will be protection for him from the Shaytan for that day, until evening comes. No one could achieve any better than him except the one who does more than he did"* (narrated by al-Bukhaari, 31119; Muslim, 2691).

لَا إِلَهَ إِلَّا اللَّهُ وَحْدَهُ لَا شَرِيكَ لَهُ لَهُ الْمُلْكُ وَلَهُ الْحَمْدُ وَهُوَ عَلَى

كُلِّ شَيْءٍ قَدِيرٌ

"Laa ilaaha ill-Allah wahdahu laa shareeka lah, lahu'l-mulk wa lahu'l-hamd wa huwa Ala kulli shay'in qadeer

"There is no God except Allah with no partner or associate; His is the Sovereignty and His is the praise, and He is able to do all things)".

18 Islamic Guidelines in Treating Physical Ailments

This chapter summarizes duas that the prophet (s.a.w.) taught the believers for the alleviation of physical pains. It should be noted that other than the duas mentioned in this chapter, scholars also use Quranic ruqyah mentioned in earlier chapters to treat general types of physical ailments and conditions. For example, Imam Ibn Al-Qayyim mentions in his famous book *"Attib un Nabawi" (Prophetic Medicine)* about reciting Quranic ruqyah in women's labor situations to alleviate their pain.

Ayesha reported that "…when the prophet (s.a.w.) complained (about pain), he would recite Mu'wadaitain and blow on himself and if it (the ailment) became severe, I would recite and would wipe his body using his hands for the blessings in them (hands)" – (Narrated by Nisai, The book of seeking protection from evil eye, #544)

A hadith that was narrated from Uthmaan ibn Abil-Aas states that he complained to the Messenger of Allah (s.a.w.) about a pain in his body. The Messenger of Allah (s.a.w.) said to him: *"Put your hand on the part of the body that hurts and say Bismillaah (in the name of Allah) three times. And say seven times: A'oodhu Billaahi wa qudratihi min sharri ma ajid wa uhaadhir (I seek refuge in Allah and His power, from the evil of what I feel and worry about)."*

بِسْمِ اللَّهِ

أَعُوذُ بِعِزَّةِ اللَّهِ، وَقُدْرَتِهِ مِنْ شَرِّ مَا أَجِدُ، وَأُحَاذِرُ،

Source: Narrated by Muslim, 2202.

Ibn Al-Qayyim states in his works about the special effects of reciting surah Al-Faatihah when he faced physical pains and ailments. He stated that during his long stay in Makkah he suffered from physical problems that no doctor or medicine could alleviate. In such cases, he would treat himself with al-Faatihah and he observed miraculous results. For this reason he used to prescribe it to whomever complained of pain, and many of them would quickly recover (Zaad Al-Maa'd 4/178, P-21 and awab Al-Kafi).

Ibn Al-Qayyim also mentioned the guidance of the prophet (s.a.w.) regarding incantations for ulcers and wounds and he mentioned the narration which is in the Saheehayn, in which it is stated that the prophet (s.a.w.) said:

"If a person is complaining of something, or he has an ulcer or a sore, he should recite with his finger thus." And Sufyan placed his finger on the ground, and then he raised it and said:

بِسْمِ اللَّهِ تُرْبَةُ أَرْضِنَا بِرِيقَةِ بَعْضِنَا يُشْفَى سَقِيمُنَا بِإِذْنِ رَبِّنَا

Bismillahi, Turbatu Ardina Bireeqati Ba'dina, Yushfa Saqeemuna Bi'idhni Rabbina

Source: Al Bukhari MaA alFatah 206/10 #5745, Muslim 1724/4 # 2194.

It was narrated from 'Aa'ishah (may Allah be pleased with her) that when the Messenger of Allah (s.a.w.) came to a sick person or when a sick person was brought to him, he would say:

143

اللَّهُمَّ أَذْهِبِ الْبَأْسَ رَبَّ النَّاسِ ، وَاشْفِ أَنْتَ الشَّافِي ، لَا شِفَاءَ إِلَّا

شِفَاؤُكَ شِفَاءً لَا يُغَادِرُ سَقَمًا

"Allah-humma adhhib il-ba's, Rabb Al-naas, washfi anta Al-Shaafi laa shifaaA illa shifaa'uka shifaaAn laa yughaadiru saqaman"

"O Allah, Lord of mankind! It is You Who removes suffering. You are the healer, and none can heal but You. I beg You to bring about healing that leaves behind no ailment."

Source: Narrated by al-Bukhaari, 5351, Muslim, 2191.

When suffering from any ailment, another dua prescribed by the prophet (s.a.w.) is the following:

أَسْأَلُ اللَّهَ الْعَظِيمَ رَبَّ الْعَرْشِ الْعَظِيمِ أَنْ يَشْفِيَكَ

As'alAllahu Al-Azeem Rabb-al-Arsh Al-Azeem a'n Yashfeek.

"I ask Allah the High, Lord of the Magnificent throne that He heals you."

Source: Abu Dawood 187/3 # 3106, Tirmidhi 410/2 # 2083, Sahah albani fi saheeh al Jamiah 180/5 - 322و ‹, Saheeh Sunan Abu Dawood 276/2)

19 Ruqyah Guidelines

The following is a summary of key guidelines that scholars have recommended for performing ruqyah.

1) Both the raaqi (the one performing ruqyah) and the patient must be in a state of cleanliness.

2) They should face the Qiblah before performing the ruqyah.

3) They must believe in the power of Allah's words and more importantly believe that healing comes only from Allah.

4) If some of the Quranic verses appear to have an effect on the patient, then those verses should be repeated 3, 5, or more times (preferably in odd numbers.)

5) Ruqyah should be performed multiple times if the case is known to be severe.

6) Women patients should be accompanied with their mahram (males that they can accompany in isolation per Islamic guidelines), especially when the raaqi is a non-mahram.

20 Other Duas for Well Being

Many times, we fall (or feel) sick due to the daily stresses involved in our lives. These stresses can be powerful enough to sap the energy from ourselves. This section includes duas that the prophet (s.a.w.) recommended for overall well being in various areas of our lives and to help make our affairs easy. However, the key principle that a person should know is that a person can find relief to all problems in the remembrance of Allah. He says in the Quran:

$$﴿الَّذِينَ آمَنُوا وَتَطْمَئِنُّ قُلُوبُهُم بِذِكْرِ اللَّهِ ۗ أَلَا بِذِكْرِ اللَّهِ تَطْمَئِنُّ الْقُلُوبُ﴾$$

"Those who believe [in the Oneness of Allah Islamic monotheism], and whose hearts find rest in the remembrance of Allah, verily, in the remembrance of Allah do hearts find rest" (Quran, Surah Ar-Raad, 13: 28).

20.1 Dua for Soundness in All Affairs

The following duas should be recited to ask Allah for keeping all affairs of one's life straight:

اَللَّهُمَّ أَصْلِحْ لِي دِينِي الَّذِي هُوَ عِصْمَةُ أَمْرِي, وَأَصْلِحْ لِي دُنْيَايَ الَّتِي فِيهَا مَعَاشِي, وَأَصْلِحْ لِي آخِرَتِي الَّتِي إِلَيْهَا مَعَادِي, وَاجْعَلِ الْحَيَاةَ زِيَادَةً لِي فِي كُلِّ خَيْرٍ, وَاجْعَلِ الْمَوْتَ رَاحَةً لِي مِنْ كُلِّ شَرٍّ

146

Allahumma aSliĥ lee deenee, allađee huwa iSmatu amree, wa-aSliĥ lee dunyaaya, allatee feehaa maaashee, wa-aSliĥ lee aakhiratee, allatee feeha maaadee, wa-jalil-ĥayaata ziyaadatal-lee fee kulli khair(iw), wa-jalil-mawta raĥatal-lee min kulli sharr.

"O Allah! Make good my religion, which is my sanctuary and make good my (present) world, where my livelihood is, and make good my Hereafter, where I will return. Fill my life with more of all that is good, and make my death a relief for me from all that is evil."

Source: Saheeh Muslim # 2720.

اللَّهُمَّ رَحْمَتَكَ أَرْجُو فَلَا تَكِلْنِي إِلَى نَفْسِي طَرْفَةَ عَيْنٍ، وَأَصْلِحْ لِي

شَأْنِي كُلَّهُ لَا إِلَهَ إِلَّا أَنْتَ

Allahumma raĥmataka arjuu, falaa takilnee ilaa nafsee Tarfata A'ayn, wa aSliĥLee sha'nee kullah, laa ilaaha illaa ant

"O Allah, it is Your mercy I am seeking. So, let me not give in to myself for the span of an eye's wink. Make good all my affairs. There is no God but You."

Source: Sunan Abu-Daawuud # 5090.

Ibn Al-Qayyim mentions in Zaad Al-Maad the guidance of the prophet (s.a.w.) regarding the treatment of every complaint with Divine incantations, and he mentioned in this regard the Hadeeth of Abu Dawud, narrated on the authoruity of Aby Ad-Darda, who attributed it to the prophet (s.a.w.) who said, *"If any of you complained of something, he should say:*

رَبُّنَا اللَّهُ الَّذِي فِي السَّمَاءِ

Rabbunallahul-Ladhee Fis-Sama"

"Our Lord is Allah, Who is in As-Sama (heavens)."

20.2 Duas for Depression and Anxiety and Psychological Problems

For cases of depression, anxiety, and psychological problems, one should recite the following duas:

اللَّهُمَّ إِنِّي أَعُوذُ بِكَ مِنْ الْهَمِّ وَالْحَزَنِ، وَالْعَجْزِ وَالْكَسَلِ، وَالْبُخْلِ وَالْجُبْنِ، وَضَلَعِ الدَّيْنِ وَغَلَبَةِ الرِّجَالِ

Allahumma inni a'oodhoo bika minal-hammi walhazni, wal-'ajzi wal-kasali wal-bukhli wal-jubni, wa dal'id-dayni wa ghalabatir rajaal

"O Allah, I seek refuge in you from anxiety and depression, from incapacity, from sloth, from miserliness, from cowardice, from the burden of debt and from being persecuted."

Source: Hadith Abu Dawood.

لَا إِلَهَ إِلَّا اللَّهُ الْعَظِيمُ الْحَلِيمُ، لَا إِلَهَ إِلَّا اللَّهُ رَبُّ الْعَرْشِ الْعَظِيمِ، لَا إِلَهَ إِلَّا اللَّهُ رَبُّ السَّمَوَاتِ، وَرَبُّ الْأَرْضِ، وَرَبُّ الْعَرْشِ الْكَرِيمِ

Laa ilaaha illal-laah-ul-aŽeem-ul-ĥaleem,laa ilaaha illal-laahu rabbul-Arshil-aŽeem,laa ilaaha illal-laahu rabbus-samaawaat (i),wa-rabbul-arD (i),wa-rabbul- Aarshil-kareem

"There is no God but Allah, the magnificent, the forbearing; there is no God but Allah, Lord of the Glorious Throne; there is no God but Allah, Lord of the heavens and the earth."

Source: Saheeh Al-Bukhari # 6346.

Another Dua that can be recited in times of hardship is the following. This was recited by Prophet Yunus (Jonah) when he was swallowed by the whale:

لا إِلَهَ إِلا أَنْتَ سُبْحَانَكَ إِنِّي كُنْتُ مِنَ الظَّالِمِينَ

Laa ilaaha illa anta, subhaanaka, inni kuntu min Al-zaalimeen

"None has the right to be worshipped but You (O Allah), glorified (and exalted) be You [above all that (evil) they associate with You]! Truly, I have been of the wrongdoers)" [Surah Al-Anbiyaa, 21:87]."

(Tirmidhi 529/5 #3505, wa alhakim, wa sahah wa wafiqh al dhahbi 505/1, wa sahah albani fi saheeh Tirmidhi 168/3)

اللَّهُ اللَّهُ رَبِّي، لاَ أُشْرِكُ بِهِ شَيْئاً

Allahu Allahu Rabbi, la ushriku bihi shaeea (a)

"Allah, Allah, He is my Lord. I do not associate anyone with Him."

Source: Sunan Abu-Daawuud, Hadith No. 1525, & Musnad Al-Imam Ahmad, Hadith No. 6/369.

According to a saheeh hadeeth narrated from Ibn Masood, the prophet (s.a.w.) promises that that if there is one who is afflicted by distress and grief, and if he says the following dua, Allah will take away his distress and grief.

اللَّهُمَّ إِنِّي عَبْدُكَ وَابْنُ عَبْدِكَ، نَاصِيَتِي بِيَدِكَ، مَاضٍ فِيَّ حُكْمُكَ،

عَدْلٌ فِيَّ قَضَاؤُكَ، أَسْأَلُكَ بِكُلِّ اسْمٍ هُوَ لَكَ، سَمَّيْتَ بِهِ نَفْسَكَ،

أَوْ عَلَّمْتَهُ أَحَداً مِنْ خَلْقِكَ، أَوْ أَنْزَلْتَهُ فِي كِتَابِكَ، أَوِ اسْتَأْثَرْتَ بِهِ

فِي عِلْمِ الْغَيْبِ عِنْدَكَ: أَنْ تَجْعَلَ الْقُرْآنَ رَبِيعَ قَلْبِي، وَنُورَ صَدْرِي،

وَجِلَاءَ حُزْنِي، وَذَهَابَ هَمِّي

Allahumma innee abduk (a) wa-bnu bdik (a), naaSiyaatee bi-yadik (a), maaDin fiyya ĥukmuk (a), adlun fiyya qaDaa-uk, as'aluka bikullismin huwalak (a), sammayta bihi nafsak (a), aw allamtahu aĥadam-minkhalaqik (a), aw-anzaltahu fee kitaabik (a), aw-ista'thart (a), bihi fee ilmil-ghaybi indak (a), antajal-alquraana rabeea qalbee, wa nuura SaDree, wa-jilaa'a ĥuznee, wa đahaaba hammee

"O Allah, I am your slave, the son of your slave. My forehead is in Your hand. Your judgment of me is inescapable. Your trial of me is just. I am invoking You by all the names that You call Yourself, that You have taught to anyone in Your creation, that You have mentioned in Your Book, or that You have kept unknown. Let the Quran be the delight of my heart, the light of my chest, the remover of my sadness and the pacifier of my worries."

Source: Musnad Ahmad # 1/391.

21 Coping with Life's Trials, Hardships, and Afflictions

The life of this world is full of hardships and trials and hoping to have a life free of troubles is to expect the impossible. It would only be in the Hereafter where the righteous among us now will enjoy a life free of troubles and problems of this world. But while in this world, we have to face various challenges in our day to day lives. Ibn Mas'ood (may Allah be pleased with him) said: *"For every moment of joy there is a moment of sorrow, and no house is filled with joy but it will be filled with sorrow."* And Ibn Sireen said: *"There is never any laughter but there comes weeping after it (islamqa.info)."*

Ailments such as sihr (witchcraft), evil eye, and other such diseases are some of the trials that Allah puts the believers through, in the course of their lives. While there are remedies for such challenges, we should also have the proper attitude of dealing with such and other challenges in life. Such a positive attitude would not only minimize the associated physical and mental stress but can aid in faster recovery from all kinds of ailments as well. That is because Allah is happy with those people who handle their difficulties with patience rather than those that adopt an attitude of complaints and ingratitude. A Muslim should believe that all that happens is by the will of Allah and an illness or a disease could either be a test from Allah or a punishment for evil deeds, which one should immediately follow up by repenting to Allah. Every test that a person goes through in this life happens by the decree of Allah, and this realization is the foremost in helping us to tackle our trials and hardships much more effectively.

Consider the following verses from the Quran:

﴿وَلَنَبْلُوَنَّكُم بِشَيْءٍ مِّنَ الْخَوْفِ وَالْجُوعِ وَنَقْصٍ مِّنَ الْأَمْوَالِ وَالْأَنفُسِ وَالثَّمَرَاتِ ۗ وَبَشِّرِ الصَّابِرِينَ﴾

﴿الَّذِينَ إِذَا أَصَابَتْهُم مُّصِيبَةٌ قَالُوا إِنَّا لِلَّهِ وَإِنَّا إِلَيْهِ رَاجِعُونَ﴾

﴿أُولَٰئِكَ عَلَيْهِمْ صَلَوَاتٌ مِّن رَّبِّهِمْ وَرَحْمَةٌ ۖ وَأُولَٰئِكَ هُمُ الْمُهْتَدُونَ﴾

- *"And certainly, We shall test you with something of fear, hunger, loss of wealth, lives and fruits, but give glad tidings to As- Saabiroon (the patient).*
- *Who, when afflicted with calamity, say: 'Truly, to Allah we belong and truly, to Him we shall return.'*
- *They are those on whom are the Salawaat (i.e. who are blessed and will be forgiven) from their Lord, and (they are those who) receive His Mercy, and it is they who are the guided ones" [Surah Al-Baqarah, 2:155-157].*

The next two sections summarize how Allah's prophets handled calamities, and underline certain steps a person can follow in handling life's challenges and calamities.

21.1 The Burdern of Sins

While it is true that Allah can test the righteous amongst us by putting us through trials and difficulties, more often than not our sins may be at the root of our dire situations. Therefore, understanding the topic of "sins" and how they can contribute to our difficulties is vital for us to address the root causes of our life's problems. The better we understand the ghastly nature of our sins, and the rate at which we accumulate them, along with their undesirable impact on our daily lives and on the life in the hereafter, the more it can propel us away from committing sins and can drive us to seek forgiveness for our sins – through making the right duas for us and for others.

Ibn Al-Qayyim provided one of the great descriptions of sins and the impact of sins in this life and the hereafter. Here is a very short summary of what he compiled about how our sins impact our lives [islamqa.info]:

- Sins deprive a person of provision (rizq) in this life. In Musnad Ahmad, it is narrated that Thawbaan said: "The Messenger of Allah (SAWS) said: 'A man is deprived of provision because of the sins that he commits'" (Narrated by Ibn Maajah, 4022, classed as hasan by al-Albaani in Saheeh Ibn Maajah).
- A sinful person experiences a sense of alienation (indifference) from his Lord, and even from other people around him. One of the salaf had said that he could see the impact of disobedience to Allah in some aspects of his daily life.
- A person who commits sins finds things becoming difficult for him. In any matter that he turns to, he finds the way blocked or very difficult to pursue. By the same token, for the one who fears Allah, things are made easy.
- 'Abd-Allah ibn 'Abbaas said: "Good deeds make the face light, give light to the heart, and bring about ample provision, physical strength and love in people's hearts. Bad deeds make the face dark, give darkness to the heart, and bring about physical weakness, a lack of provision and hatred in people's hearts."
- Sins breed sins, until it dominates a person and he cannot escape from it. Sins weaken a person's willpower. It gradually strengthens his will to keep committing sins and

weakens his will to repent, until there is no will in his heart to repent at all. Thus, even when he seeks forgiveness from Allah and expresses repentance, it is merely words on the lips, like the repentance of the liars, whose hearts are still determined to commit sins and persist in it. This is one of the most serious diseases, which may lead a person to doom because he becomes so desensitized that he no longer finds sins abhorrent; thus it becomes his habit, and he is not bothered, if people see him committing a sin or talk about his sinful ways of life.

So, we can easily see that by engaging in sins, we are not only making the prospects of our hereafter (an integral part of Islamic faith) bleak; but sins can greatly and actively contribute to the difficulties of our daily lives as well. Allah says in the Quran:

$$\text{﴿مَّا أَصَابَكَ مِنْ حَسَنَةٍ فَمِنَ اللَّهِ ۖ وَمَا أَصَابَكَ مِن سَيِّئَةٍ فَمِن نَّفْسِكَ ۚ﴾}$$

"Whatever of good reaches you, is from Allah, but whatever of evil befalls you, is from yourself..." [Surah al-Nisa, 4:79]

Whether we encounter challenges in earning a living, or in our family affairs, or in other matters of life, the burden of sins greatly inhibits us from seeking the ultimate blessings of Allah and makes it impossible to lead a pure life in this world.

21.2 Handling of Calamities by the Prophets

The Quran highlights numerous examples that show the prophets and the pious were tested for their strong faiths in Allah. Those verses also prove that the pious will continue to be tested by Allah as He pleases. In this context, a hadith by Al-Tirmidhi (2398) narrates that Saa'd ibn Abi Waqqaas (may Allah be pleased with him) said:

> 'I said: "O Messenger of Allah, which of the people are most sorely tested?" He said: "The prophets, then the next best and the next best. A man will be tested in accordance with his level of religious commitment. If his religious commitment is strong, he will be tested more severely, and if his religious commitment is weak, he will be tested in accordance with his religious commitment. Calamity will keep befalling a person until he walks on the earth with no sin on him."' [Classed as saheeh by Al-Albaani in Al-Silsilah Al-Saheehah, 143.]

As Muslims, we should learn how to handle life's challenges from what Allah has informed us in the Quran and how the prophet (s.a.w.) taught us through his words and actions. The Quran and hadith narrate a number of such incidents that reveal how the prophets handled various calamities in their lives and how Allah described their situations, so that we could follow in their footsteps.

Consider the story of Prophet Ayyub (a.s.) who lost all his wealth, children, and health. Yet, he remained steadfast and Allah eventually returned him everything he had lost. Allah said about Ayyub,

$$﴿إِنَّا وَجَدْنَاهُ صَابِرًا ۚ نِعْمَ الْعَبْدُ ۖ إِنَّهُ أَوَّابٌ﴾$$

"...We found him patient. How excellent a slave! Verily he was ever oft-returning in repentance (to Us)!" (Quran, Surah Saad, 38: 44)

Prophet Ibraheem (a.s.) was asked by Allah to take his wife and new born child and leave them in the desert with no water and food. He was also asked to sacrifice his son, Ismaeel. As a token of being steadfast, Allah took Prophet Ibraheem as His "Khaleel" (friend). Allah also said about Prophet Ibraheem:

﴾سَلَامٌ عَلَىٰ إِبْرَاهِيمَ﴿

"Salam (peace) be upon Ibrahim (Abraham)!" (Quran, Surah As-Saaffat, 37: 109)

Similarly, we have read about the life of Prophet Yusuf (a.s.) in the holy Quran, how he was thrown in a well by his brothers at a young age and was later imprisoned in his adulthood. Allah later rewarded him by making him the King of Egypt. Prophet Yusuf then made the following Dua as mentioned in the Quran:

﴾رَبِّ قَدْ آتَيْتَنِي مِنَ الْمُلْكِ وَعَلَّمْتَنِي مِن تَأْوِيلِ الْأَحَادِيثِ

فَاطِرَ السَّمَاوَاتِ وَالْأَرْضِ أَنتَ وَلِيِّي فِي الدُّنْيَا وَالْآخِرَةِ

تَوَفَّنِي مُسْلِمًا وَأَلْحِقْنِي بِالصَّالِحِينَ﴿

"My Lord! You have indeed bestowed on me of the sovereignty, and taught me something of the interpretation of dreams – the (Only) Creator of the heavens and the earth! You are my Wali (Protector, Helper, Supporter, Guardian, God, Lord) in this world and in the Hereafter. Cause me to die as a Muslim (the one submitting to Your Will), and join me with the righteous" (Quran, Surah Yousuf, 12: 101)

These are only some of the incidents related to the ordeals of the prophets and righteous people. In our day-to-day lives, most of us probably observe similar trials in our own or in other people's lives. We should take heed from such lessons and mould our attitudes by constantly asking Allah for forgiveness of our sins, by remembering Allah's power and decree, by reminding ourselves about the temporary nature of this life, and by never giving up hope in Allah and His rewards.

As we noticed in the story of Prophet Ayyub (a.s.), we may be tested according to the level of our faith in anything that we may possess. That may include our wealth, assets, health, or other possessions. Allah says in the Quran:

$$﴿لَتُبْلَوُنَّ فِي أَمْوَالِكُمْ وَأَنفُسِكُمْ وَلَتَسْمَعُنَّ مِنَ الَّذِينَ أُوتُوا الْكِتَابَ مِن قَبْلِكُمْ وَمِنَ الَّذِينَ أَشْرَكُوا أَذًى كَثِيرًا ۚ وَإِن تَصْبِرُوا وَتَتَّقُوا فَإِنَّ ذَٰلِكَ مِنْ عَزْمِ الْأُمُورِ﴾$$

"You shall certainly be tried and tested in your wealth and properties and in your personal selves, and you shall certainly hear much that will grieve you from those who received the Scripture before you and from those who ascribe partners to Allah; but if you persevere patiently, and become Al-Muttaqun (the pious) then verily, that will be a determining factor in all affairs (and that is from the great matters which you must hold on with all your efforts) (Surah Aal-e-Imran, 3: 186).

21.3 Handling Calamities and Challenges in Life

In the earlier section, we observed how the prophets, who were Allah's chosen people, were afflicted by calamities and trials and how they handled those calamities. This section summarizes some key strategies that can help us in handling calamities that we are likely to face in our lives. If we follow these guidelines strictly, we will find ourselves among those whom Allah has praised in the Quran. As we observed earlier, Allah mentioned this about Prophet Ayuub (A.S.):

$$﴿إِنَّا وَجَدْنَاهُ صَابِرًا ۚ نِّعْمَ الْعَبْدُ ۖ إِنَّهُ أَوَّابٌ﴾$$

"...We found him patient. How excellent a slave! Verily he was ever oft-returning in repentance (to Us)!" (Quran, Surah Saad, 38: 44)

The following is a summary of the various practices that can help one in coping with calamities and challenges in life.

21.3.1 Exercising Patience

One of the most important aspects of handling calamities in life is exercising patience. When one handles his or her calamities with patience and absolute belief in Allah, He rewards that individual in many ways, both in this life and in the hereafter. The prophet (s.a.w.) said in a hadith:

$$إِذَا ابْتَلَيْتُ عَبْدِي بِحَبِيبَتَيْهِ فَصَبَرَ [وَاحْتَسَبَ] عَوَّضْتُهُ$$

$$مِنْهُمَا الْجَنَّةَ ۚ$$

If I tested my slave involving his loved ones (i.e. his/her death)and he showed patience and was sure of the reward in the hereafter, I will reward him Jannah for them (patience and expectation of reward.
[Source: Bukhari Al Fath 116/10 # 5653, Saheeh Tirmidhi 286/2.]

Patience in this context means refraining from complaints and being satisfied with the divine decree. We can exercise patience by reminding ourselves that Allah tests us in our times of hardship. Among the many things He tests us with are the level of our belief in Him and in His message of truth, our demeanor in handling our ordeals (how we treat ourselves and others), and whether we stay steadfast in asking for His mercy. The stories of the prophets tell us that their ordeals sometimes lasted for years but that did not let them lose patience, which, in turn, shows that they were grounded in their belief in Allah. Prophet Nooh (peace be upon him) remained among his people for 950 years and was accused and resisted. The prophets Yaqoob and Yoosuf (peace be upon them) were tested with a lengthy separation spanned over many years that led to Prophet Yaqoob's (peace be upon him) blindness. Prophets Zakariya and Yahya (peace be upon them) resisted the torments of their people until they were killed by them. The people of Prophet 'Eesa (peace be upon him) wanted to crucify him but Allah raised him to Himself. Prophet Muhammad (s.a.w.) was expelled by his people from his land; they reviled him and insulted him and wanted to kill him; but he remained steadfast and patient until Allah made him victorious.

By learning about the difficult situations of the prophets, we can try to put our problems in the right perspective and deal with them in the same manner as they did. We can derive strength and courage from their experiences and try to handle the problems of our lives with conviction and determination.

21.3.2 Belief in the Divine Decree

The belief that all ordeals are decreed by Allah can help an individual to handle the calamity he may face with patience. After all, no one loves His creation more than Allah Himself – the Creator – and if the Creator wills a calamity on His creation, then no one can ward it off.

Allah says in the Quran:

$$\text{مَا أَصَابَ مِنْ مُصِيبَةٍ إِلَّا بِإِذْنِ اللَّهِ وَمَنْ يُؤْمِنْ بِاللَّهِ يَهْدِ قَلْبَهُ وَاللَّهُ بِكُلِّ شَيْءٍ عَلِيمٌ}$$

"No calamity befalls, but by the Leave [i.e. Decision and Qadar (Divine Preordainments)] of Allah, and whosoever believes in Allah, He guides his heart [to the true Faith

with certainty, i.e. what has befallen him was already written for him by Allah from the Qadar (Divine Preordainments)]. And Allah is the All-Knower of everything" (Surah Taghabun, 64, 11).

When facing difficulties, our weak faith can sometimes drive us to question the fairness of it all. In this context, we should remind ourselves that believing in al-Qadr (Allah's divine will and decree) is one of the pillars of Islamic faith. As the prophet (s.a.w.) said, the pillars of Islamic faith include belief in: (1) Allah, (2) His Angels, (3) His revealed Holy Books (Quran, Bible, Torah, etc.), (4) His Messengers, (5) the Day of Judgment, and (6) al-Qadar (the divine decree) – both good and bad.

Allah also says in the Quran,

$$\text{﴾مَا أَصَابَ مِنْ مُصِيبَةٍ فِي الْأَرْضِ وَلَا فِي أَنْفُسِكُمْ إِلَّا فِي كِتَابٍ مِنْ قَبْلِ أَنْ نَبْرَأَهَا إِنَّ ذَلِكَ عَلَى اللَّهِ يَسِيرٌ * لِكَيْ لَا تَأْسَوْا عَلَى مَا فَاتَكُمْ وَلَا تَفْرَحُوا بِمَا آتَاكُمْ وَاللَّهُ لَا يُحِبُّ كُلَّ مُخْتَالٍ فَخُورٍ﴾}$$

"No calamity befalls on the earth or in your selves but it is inscribed in the Book of Decrees (Al-Lawh Al-Mahfooz) before We bring it into existence. Verily, that is easy for Allah"

In order that you may not grieve at the things that you fail to get, nor rejoice over that which has been given to you. And Allah likes not prideful boasters.

[Surah al-Hadeed, 57:22-23].

As part of that belief, we should, therefore, recognize that Allah does what He wills for reasons that are only known to Him. Any attempt to comprehend His wisdom with our limited knowledge, or to understand how our current situation fits in His overall plan can only lead us to erroneous conclusions and perhaps more frustrations.

Annas bin Malik narrates this as having been said by the prophet:

إِنَّ عِظَمَ الْجَزَاءِ مَعَ عِظَمِ الْبَلَاءِ, وَإِنَّ اللهَ إِذَا أَحَبَّ قَوْمًا

ابْتَلَاهُمْ, فَمَنْ رَضِيَ فَلَهُ الرِّضَا, وَمَنْ سَخِطَ فَلَهُ السَّخَطُ

"The greatness of reward is based on the severity of the trial. And if Allah loves a person, he tests him, so whoever is pleased (with Allah and His decree), then he will have the pleasure (of Allah), but whoever is angry, then he will receive the anger (of Allah)."

[Source: Tirmidhi # 2396, Ibn Majah # 4031]

21.3.3 Knowing that Everything will Come to an End

We should remember that nothing in this world is meant to last indefinitely and everything eventually has to come to an end. All mortals will have to die one day, and their joys and sorrows will also end with their lives. We cannot, therefore, expect everything to stay perfect forever. Allah says in the Quran:

﴿كُلُّ شَيْءٍ هَالِكٌ إِلَّا وَجْهَهُ ۚ لَهُ الْحُكْمُ وَإِلَيْهِ تُرْجَعُونَ﴾

"...Everything will perish except His Face. His is the Decision, and to Him you (all) shall be returned" (Surah Al-Qasas, 28: 88).

The best a person can do is to remember that we came from Allah, and to Him we will return. Muslim narrated in his Saheeh (1525) that Umm Salamah said: I heard the Messenger of Allah (s.a.w.) say,

$$\text{مَا مِنْ عَبْدٍ تُصِيبُهُ مُصِيبَةٌ، فَيَقُولُ: إِنَّا للهِ وَإِنَّا إِلَيْهِ رَاجِعُونَ،}$$

$$\text{اللَّهُمَّ أَجُرْنِي فِي مُصِيبَتِي، وَأَخْلِفْ لِي خَيْراً مِنْهَا، إِلاَّ أَجَرَهُ}$$

$$\text{اللهُ تَعَالَى فِي مُصِيبَتِهِ، وَأَخْلَفَ لَهُ خَيْراً مِنْهَا}$$

"There is no Muslim who is afflicted with a calamity and says that which Allaah has enjoined, Innaa lillaahi wa inna ilayhi raaji'oon. Allaahumma ajurni fi museebati wakhluf li khayran minha (Verily to Allaah we belong and unto Him is our return. O Allaah, reward me for my calamity and compensate me with something better than it), but Allaah will compensate him with something better than it."

21.3.4 Staying Clear of the "If-Only" Trap

Another trap that many of us fall into is using the "if-only" logic. Very often, our minds tell us that "if I could have done such and such, then this wouldn't have happened." The prophet warned us against falling into such satanic traps. In a hadith narrated by Abu Hurayrah, the prophet remarked,

> "... If anything befalls you, do not say 'If only I had done (such and such), then such and such would have happened,' rather say: 'Allah has decreed and what He wills He does,' for 'if only' opens the door to the work of the Shaytan (Satan)." Narrated by Muslim (2664).

We see another example of this during the battle of Uhud when many Muslims died. This gave the hypocrites an excuse to criticize the divine decree. But Allah refuted their claims by stating:

قُل لَّوْ كُنتُمْ فِي بُيُوتِكُمْ لَبَرَزَ الَّذِينَ كُتِبَ عَلَيْهِمُ الْقَتْلُ إِلَىٰ مَضَاجِعِهِمْ

"Say: 'Even if you had remained in your homes, those for whom death was decreed would certainly have gone forth to the place of their death'" [Surah Aal-e-Imraan, 3:154].

This further goes on to show that what Allah decrees is inevitable. Any attempt to imagine a different outcome based on a different set of actions that we could have taken has no merit in Islam and will only increase our frustration. This belief in Allah is also a blessing because it prevents us from recalling the past that can result in nothing but an added emotional baggage.

21.3.5 Remembering Allah and Seeking Constant Forgiveness

One of the main reasons why calamities befall human beings could be their involvement in sins. The Quran and hadith provide many references to calamities, their link to our sins, and how calamities rid us of our sins. Consider the following:

Allah says in the Quran:

وَمَا أَصَابَكُم مِّن مُّصِيبَةٍ فَبِمَا كَسَبَتْ أَيْدِيكُمْ وَيَعْفُو عَن كَثِيرٍ

"And whatever misfortune befalls you, it is because of what your hands have earned. And He pardons much. Quran." (Surah Ash-Shura, 42: 30)

A person, therefore, should constantly ask for Allah's forgiveness, as acceptance of one's forgiveness may provide a person a way out of his calamity, whether it is from an ailment or a disease or other troubles. We should ask for repentance from every sin no matter how large or small. Even small sins can accumulate to push us into problems. Abd-Allah ibn Mas'ood reported that the Messenger of Allah (s.a.w.) said:

"Beware of sins that are seen as insignificant, for they will keep accumulating until they destroy a man." The Messenger of Allah (s.a.w.) explained this by comparing them to people who stop to camp in the wilderness and decide to build a fire, so one man goes out and brings back a stick, and another man brings a stick, until they have gathered enough, then they light a fire and cook whatever they throw onto it (Reported by Ahmad, 1/402; al-Silsilat al-Saheehah, 389).

The prophet drew a similarity between the collection of sticks and our small sins, which keep accumulating if we keep collecting them, to an extent that they become enough to light a fire. Seeking forgiveness for our sins constantly, therefore, may potentially rid us of that burden on an ongoing basis. The prophet (s.a.w.) also said:

"Whoever does a lot of Istighfar, Allah will provide him a way out of each concern he has, and will solve all his troubles, and will provide him with livelihood from sources that were not known to him" (Narrated by Imam Ahmad, Sanad Saheeh.)

21.3.6 Not to Overly Attach Oneself with the Attractions of this Life

Hardships and trials also remind us not to overly attach ourselves with what this world has to offer. The more attached we are to certain things in life, the more we feel the loss of such assets. Coping with the loss of material things in this world becomes even more difficult if we start believing that living our lives without such things is not possible. We may associate happiness with material objects and upon losing these, we often get disheartened. The teachings of Islam remind us that the greatest affliction is to lose Allah's mercy in the hereafter. Allah reminds us in the Quran that on the Day of Judgement the true losers will be those who lose not just themselves but also their families. Consider this verse in the Quran:

وَقَالَ الَّذِينَ آمَنُوا إِنَّ الْخَاسِرِينَ الَّذِينَ خَسِرُوا أَنفُسَهُمْ

وَأَهْلِيهِمْ يَوْمَ الْقِيَامَةِ

'And those who believe will say: "Verily, the losers are they who lose themselves and their families on the Day of Resurrection' (Surah Ash-Shura, 42: 45).

21.3.7 Staying Focused on the Mercy of Allah

As believers, we should never lose hope in the mercy of Allah because the only thing that can relieve us of our life's burdens is His mercy. Adhering to this belief and doing everything possible to attain His mercy can help us relieve the burden of our challenges and problems.

Allah says in the Quran:

قُلْ يَا عِبَادِيَ الَّذِينَ أَسْرَفُوا عَلَىٰ أَنفُسِهِمْ لَا تَقْنَطُوا مِن

رَّحْمَةِ اللَّهِ ۚ إِنَّ اللَّهَ يَغْفِرُ الذُّنُوبَ جَمِيعًا ۚ إِنَّهُ هُوَ الْغَفُورُ

الرَّحِيمُ

Say: O My servants who have transgressed against their own souls, despair not of the mercy of Allah. Indeed, Allah forgives all sins. Truly, He is Most Forgiving, Most Merciful (Surah az-Zumar, 39:53).

The prophet (s.a.w.) said in a hadith Qudsi that Allah says:

"O son of Adam, as long as you call upon Me and put your hope in Me, I have forgiven you for what you have done and I do not mind. O son of Adam, if your sins were to reach the clouds of the sky and then you would seek My forgiveness, I would forgive you. O son of Adam, if you were to come to Me with sins that are close to filling the earth and then you would meet Me without ascribing any partners with Me, I would certainly bring to you forgiveness close to filling it." (Hadith Qudsi)

21.3.8 Thinking of Allah's Blessings on Us

Even in times of hardship, we should never cease to think of Allah's many blessings on us. Our plight may be a tough one, but we should never fall in a state where we feel sorry for ourselves. Instead, we should turn our attention to the many blessings that Allah has granted us and that others do not have. Adopting this attitude of gratitude can help us raise our status in the eyes of Allah, Who in turn can find us a way through our troubles, if He wills it so. By remembering His blessings, we can make a paradigm shift in our thinking because this way we shall focus on the positive things in our life instead of worrying about our problems. Such positive attitude would automatically strengthen our belief in Allah and would minimize the sense of loss and deprivation, which may have resulted from the hardships and difficulties of life.

21.3.9 Knowing that Allah Forgives Sins in Times of Calamity

We should also remember that the onset of a calamity results in the forgiving of one's sins. In a popular hadith, the prophet (s.a.w.) said,

مَا مِنْ مُسْلِمٍ يُصِيبُهُ أَذًى: مِنْ مَرَضٍ فَمَا سِوَاهُ إِلَّا حَطَّ اللَّهُ

بِهِ سَيِّئَاتِهِ كَمَا تَحُطُّ الشَّجَرَةُ وَرَقَهَا

" *No Muslim is afflicted with hurt caused by disease or some other inconvenience, but that Allah will remove his sins as a tree sheds its leaves.*" [Source: Bukhari Al Fath 120/10 # 5684, Muslim 1991/4 # 2571]

We also know that Allah rejoices when we repent to Him for our sins. *According to a hadith narrated by Muslim (2747), "Allah rejoices more over the repentance of His slave than any one of you if he is on his camel in a desolate land, then it runs away from him and on it is his food and drink, and he despairs of finding it, so he goes to a tree and lies down in its shade, having despaired of finding his camel, then while he is like that, it suddenly appears in front of him and he takes hold of its reins and says, because of his intense joy, 'O Allah, You are my slave and I am your lord,' making this mistake because of the intensity of his joy."*

22 Appendix I – 37 Verses with "La Ilaha IllAllah"

For ruqyah treatments, scholars have also used the following 37 verses of the Quran. These verses contain the words "La Ilaha Illa-Allah". As we know from ahadith that the words La Ilaha IllAllah are heavier than everyting that is in the heavens and the earth. As these verses are part of the Quran, their recitation is used in many ruqyah treatments as well.

So know (O Muhammad صلى الله عليه وسلم) that, La ilaha illallah (none has the right to be worshipped but Allah), and ask forgiveness for your sin, and also for (the sin of) believing men and believing women. And Allah knows well your moving about, and your place of rest (in your homes). Surah Al-Muhammad, 47: 19	فَاعْلَمْ أَنَّهُ لَا إِلَهَ إِلَّا اللَّهُ وَاسْتَغْفِرْ لِذَنبِكَ وَلِلْمُؤْمِنِينَ وَالْمُؤْمِنَاتِ ۗ وَاللَّهُ يَعْلَمُ مُتَقَلَّبَكُمْ وَمَثْوَاكُمْ
Truly, when it was said to them: La ilaha illallah "(none has the right to be worshipped but Allah)," they puffed themselves up with pride (i.e. denied it). And (they) said: "Are we going to abandon our alihah (gods) for the sake of a mad poet?" Surah Al-Saffat, 37: 35-36	إِنَّهُمْ كَانُوا إِذَا قِيلَ لَهُمْ لَا إِلَهَ إِلَّا اللَّهُ يَسْتَكْبِرُونَ*وَيَقُولُونَ أَئِنَّا لَتَارِكُو آلِهَتِنَا لِشَاعِرٍ مَّجْنُونٍ

till when drowning overtook him, he said: "I believe that none has the right to be worshipped but He (Allah) in Whom the Children of Israel believe, and I am one of the Muslims (those who submit to Allah's Will)." Surah Al-Yunus, 10:90	حَتَّىٰ إِذَا أَدْرَكَهُ الْغَرَقُ قَالَ آمَنْتُ أَنَّهُ لَا إِلَهَ إِلَّا الَّذِي آمَنَتْ بِهِ بَنُو إِسْرَائِيلَ وَأَنَا مِنَ الْمُسْلِمِينَ
He sends down the angels with the Ruh (revelation) of His Command to whom of His slaves He wills (saying): "Warn mankind that La ilaha illa Ana (none has the right to be worshipped but I), so fear Me (by abstaining from sins and evil deeds). Surah Al-Nahl, 16:2	يُنَزِّلُ الْمَلَائِكَةَ بِالرُّوحِ مِنْ أَمْرِهِ عَلَىٰ مَن يَشَاءُ مِنْ عِبَادِهِ أَنْ أَنذِرُوا أَنَّهُ لَا إِلَهَ إِلَّا أَنَا فَاتَّقُونِ
"Verily! I am Allah! La ilaha illa Ana (none has the right to be worshipped but I), so worship Me, and perform As-Salat (Iqamat-as-Salat) for My Remembrance. Surah Al-Taha, 20:14	إِنَّنِي أَنَا اللَّهُ لَا إِلَهَ إِلَّا أَنَا فَاعْبُدْنِي وَأَقِمِ الصَّلَاةَ لِذِكْرِي
And We did not send any Messenger before you (O Muhammad صلى الله عليه وسلم) but We revealed to him (saying): La ilaha illa Ana [none has the right to be worshipped but I (Allah)], so worship Me (Alone and none else)." Surah Al-Anbiya, 21:25	وَمَا أَرْسَلْنَا مِن قَبْلِكَ مِن رَّسُولٍ إِلَّا نُوحِي إِلَيْهِ أَنَّهُ لَا إِلَهَ إِلَّا أَنَا فَاعْبُدُونِ

And (remember) Dhun-Nun (Jonah), when he went off in anger, and imagined that We shall not punish him (i.e. the calamities which had befallen him)! But he cried through the darkness (saying): La ilaha illa Anta [none has the right to be worshipped but You (O, Allah)], Glorified (and Exalted) be You [above all that (evil) they associate with You)]! Truly, I have been of the wrong-doers." Surah Al-Anbiya, 21:87	وَذَا النُّونِ إِذ ذَّهَبَ مُغَاضِبًا فَظَنَّ أَن لَّن نَّقْدِرَ عَلَيْهِ فَنَادَىٰ فِي الظُّلُمَاتِ أَن لَّا إِلَهَ إِلَّا أَنتَ سُبْحَانَكَ إِنِّي كُنتُ مِنَ الظَّالِمِينَ
And your Ilah (God) is One Ilah (God - Allah), La ilaha illa Huwa (there is none who has the right to be worshipped but He), the Most Gracious, the Most Merciful. Surah Al-Baqara, 2:163	وَإِلَهُكُمْ إِلَهٌ وَاحِدٌ ۖ لَّا إِلَهَ إِلَّا هُوَ الرَّحْمَٰنُ الرَّحِيمُ
Allah! La ilaha illa Huwa (none has the right to be worshipped but He), Al-Hayyul-Qayyum (the Ever Living, the One Who sustains and protects all that exists). Surah Al-Baqara, 2:255	اللَّهُ لَا إِلَهَ إِلَّا هُوَ الْحَيُّ الْقَيُّومُ
Alif-Lam-Mim. [These letters are one of the miracles of the Qur'an, and none but Allah (Alone) knows their meanings]. Allah! La ilaha illa Huwa (none has the right to be worshipped but He), Al-Hayyul-Qayyum (the Ever Living, the One Who sustains and protects all that exists). Surah Al-e-Imran, 3:1-2	الم*اللَّهُ لَا إِلَهَ إِلَّا هُوَ الْحَيُّ الْقَيُّومُ

He it is Who shapes you in the wombs as He wills. La ilaha illa Huwa (none has the right to be worshipped but He), the All-Mighty, the All-Wise. Surah Al-e-Imran, 3:6	هُوَ الَّذِي يُصَوِّرُكُمْ فِي الْأَرْحَامِ كَيْفَ يَشَاءُ ۚ لَا إِلَهَ إِلَّا هُوَ الْعَزِيزُ الْحَكِيمُ
Allah bears witness that La ilaha illa Huwa (none has the right to be worshipped but He), and the angels, and those having knowledge (also give this witness); (He always) maintains His creation in Justice. La ilaha illa Huwa (none has the right to be worshipped but He), the All-Mighty, the All-Wise. Surah Al-e-Imran, 3:18	شَهِدَ اللَّهُ أَنَّهُ لَا إِلَهَ إِلَّا هُوَ وَالْمَلَائِكَةُ وَأُولُو الْعِلْمِ قَائِمًا بِالْقِسْطِ ۚ لَا إِلَهَ إِلَّا هُوَ الْعَزِيزُ الْحَكِيمُ
Verily! This is the true narrative [about the story of 'Îsa (Jesus)], and La ilaha illallah (none has the right to be worshipped but Allah, the One and the Only True God, Who has neither a wife nor a son). And indeed, Allah is the All-Mighty, the All-Wise. Surah Al-e-Imran, 3:62	إِنَّ هَٰذَا لَهُوَ الْقَصَصُ الْحَقُّ ۚ وَمَا مِنْ إِلَهٍ إِلَّا اللَّهُ ۚ وَإِنَّ اللَّهَ لَهُوَ الْعَزِيزُ الْحَكِيمُ
Allah! La ilaha illa Huwa (none has the right to be worshipped but He). Surely, He will gather you together on the Day of Resurrection about which there is no doubt. And who is truer in statement than Allah? Surah An-Nisa, 4:87	اللَّهُ لَا إِلَهَ إِلَّا هُوَ ۚ لَيَجْمَعَنَّكُمْ إِلَىٰ يَوْمِ الْقِيَامَةِ لَا رَيْبَ فِيهِ ۗ وَمَنْ أَصْدَقُ مِنَ اللَّهِ حَدِيثًا

Such is Allah, your Lord! La ilaha illa Huwa (none has the right to be worshipped but He), the Creator of all things. So worship Him (Alone), and He is the Wakil (Trustee, Disposer of affairs, Guardian) over all things. Surah Al-Anaam, 6:102	ذَٰلِكُمُ اللَّهُ رَبُّكُمْ ۖ لَا إِلَٰهَ إِلَّا هُوَ ۖ خَالِقُ كُلِّ شَيْءٍ فَاعْبُدُوهُ ۚ وَهُوَ عَلَىٰ كُلِّ شَيْءٍ وَكِيلٌ
Follow what has been revealed to you (O Muhammad صلى الله عليه وسلم) from your Lord, La ilaha illa Huwa (none has the right to be worshipped but He) and turn aside from Al-Mushrikun Surah Al-Anaam, 6:106	اتَّبِعْ مَا أُوحِيَ إِلَيْكَ مِن رَّبِّكَ ۖ لَا إِلَٰهَ إِلَّا هُوَ ۖ وَأَعْرِضْ عَنِ الْمُشْرِكِينَ
Say (O Muhammad صلى الله عليه وسلم): "O mankind! Verily, I am sent to you all as the Messenger of Allah - to Whom belongs the dominion of the heavens and the earth. La ilaha illa Huwa (none has the right to be worshipped but He). It is He Who gives life and causes death. Surah Al-Araf, 7:158	قُلْ يَا أَيُّهَا النَّاسُ إِنِّي رَسُولُ اللَّهِ إِلَيْكُمْ جَمِيعًا الَّذِي لَهُ مُلْكُ السَّمَاوَاتِ وَالْأَرْضِ ۖ لَا إِلَٰهَ إِلَّا هُوَ يُحْيِي وَيُمِيتُ
They (Jews and Christians) took their rabbis and their monks to be their lords besides Allah (by obeying them in things which they made lawful or unlawful according to their own desires without being ordered by Allah), and (they also took as their Lord) Messiah, son of Maryam (Mary), while they (Jews and Christians) were commanded [in the Taurat (Torah) and the Injeel (Gospel)] to worship none but One Ilah (God - Allah) La ilaha illa Huwa (none has the right to be	اتَّخَذُوا أَحْبَارَهُمْ وَرُهْبَانَهُمْ أَرْبَابًا مِّن دُونِ اللَّهِ وَالْمَسِيحَ ابْنَ مَرْيَمَ وَمَا أُمِرُوا إِلَّا لِيَعْبُدُوا إِلَٰهًا وَاحِدًا ۖ لَّا إِلَٰهَ إِلَّا هُوَ ۚ سُبْحَانَهُ عَمَّا يُشْرِكُونَ

worshipped but He) . *Praise and glory be to Him (far above is He) from having the partners they associate (with Him)."* Surah Al-Tauba 9:31	
But if they turn away, say (O Muhammad صلى الله عليه وسلم*): "Allah is sufficient for me. La ilaha illa Huwa (none has the right to be worshipped but He) in Him I put my trust and He is the Lord of the Mighty Throne."* Surah Al-Tauba 9:129	فَإِن تَوَلَّوْا فَقُلْ حَسْبِيَ اللَّهُ لَا إِلَٰهَ إِلَّا هُوَ ۖ عَلَيْهِ تَوَكَّلْتُ ۖ وَهُوَ رَبُّ الْعَرْشِ الْعَظِيمِ
If then they answer you not, know then that it [the Revelation (this Qur'an)] is sent down with the Knowledge of Allah and that La ilaha illa Huwa: (none has the right to be worshipped but He)! Will you then be Muslims (those who submit in Islam)? Surah Al-Hud 11:14	فَإِلَّمْ يَسْتَجِيبُوا لَكُمْ فَاعْلَمُوا أَنَّمَا أُنزِلَ بِعِلْمِ اللَّهِ وَأَن لَّا إِلَٰهَ إِلَّا هُوَ ۖ فَهَلْ أَنتُم مُّسْلِمُونَ
Thus have We sent you (O Muhammad صلى الله عليه و سلم *) to a community before whom other communities have passed away, in order that you might recite unto them what We have revealed to you, while they disbelieve in the Most Gracious (Allah) Say: "He is my Lord! La ilaha illa Huwa (none has the right to be worshipped but He)! In Him is my trust, and to Him will be my return with repentance."* Surah Al-Raad 13:30	كَذَٰلِكَ أَرْسَلْنَاكَ فِي أُمَّةٍ قَدْ خَلَتْ مِن قَبْلِهَا أُمَمٌ لِّتَتْلُوَ عَلَيْهِمُ الَّذِي أَوْحَيْنَا إِلَيْكَ وَهُمْ يَكْفُرُونَ بِالرَّحْمَٰنِ ۚ قُلْ هُوَ رَبِّي لَا إِلَٰهَ إِلَّا هُوَ عَلَيْهِ تَوَكَّلْتُ وَإِلَيْهِ مَتَابِ

Allah! La ilaha illa Huwa (none has the right to be worshipped but He)! To Him belong the Best Names. Surah Al-Taha 20:8	اللَّهُ لَا إِلَهَ إِلَّا هُوَ ۚ لَهُ الْأَسْمَاءُ الْحُسْنَىٰ
Your Ilah (God) is only Allah, (the One) La ilaha illa Huwa (none has the right to be worshipped but He). He has full knowledge of all things. Surah Al-Taha 20:98	إِنَّمَا إِلَهُكُمُ اللَّهُ الَّذِي لَا إِلَهَ إِلَّا هُوَ ۚ وَسِعَ كُلَّ شَيْءٍ عِلْمًا
So Exalted be Allah, the True King: La ilaha illa Huwa (none has the right to be worshipped but He), the Lord of the Supreme Throne! Surah Al-Mumenoon 23:116	فَتَعَالَى اللَّهُ الْمَلِكُ الْحَقُّ ۗ لَا إِلَهَ إِلَّا هُوَ رَبُّ الْعَرْشِ الْكَرِيمِ
Allah, La ilaha illa Huwa (none has the right to be worshipped but He), the Lord of the Supreme Throne! Surah Al-Naml 27:26	اللَّهُ لَا إِلَهَ إِلَّا هُوَ رَبُّ الْعَرْشِ الْعَظِيمِ
And He is Allah: La ilaha illa Huwa (none has the right to be worshipped but He), all praises and thanks be to Him (both) in the first (i.e. in this world) and in the last (i.e. in the Hereafter). And for Him is the Decision, and to Him shall you (all) be returned. Surah Al-Qasas 28:70	وَهُوَ اللَّهُ لَا إِلَهَ إِلَّا هُوَ ۖ لَهُ الْحَمْدُ فِي الْأُولَىٰ وَالْآخِرَةِ ۖ وَلَهُ الْحُكْمُ وَإِلَيْهِ تُرْجَعُونَ
And invoke not any other ilah (god) along with Allah: La ilaha illa Huwa (none has the right to be worshipped but He). Everything will perish save His Face. His is the Decision, and to Him you (all) shall be returned. Surah Al-Qasas 28:88	وَلَا تَدْعُ مَعَ اللَّهِ إِلَهًا آخَرَ ۘ لَا إِلَهَ إِلَّا هُوَ ۚ كُلُّ شَيْءٍ هَالِكٌ إِلَّا وَجْهَهُ ۚ لَهُ الْحُكْمُ

	وَإِلَيْهِ تُرْجَعُونَ
Surah Al-Fatir 35:3	يَا أَيُّهَا النَّاسُ اذْكُرُوا نِعْمَتَ اللَّهِ عَلَيْكُمْ ۚ هَلْ مِنْ خَالِقٍ غَيْرُ اللَّهِ يَرْزُقُكُم مِّنَ السَّمَاءِ وَالْأَرْضِ ۚ لَا إِلَهَ إِلَّا هُوَ ۖ فَأَنَّىٰ تُؤْفَكُونَ
Such is Allah your Lord. His is the kingdom. La ilaha illa Huwa (none has the right to be worshipped but He). How then are you turned away? Surah Az-Zumar 39:6	ذَٰلِكُمُ اللَّهُ رَبُّكُمْ لَهُ الْمُلْكُ ۖ لَا إِلَهَ إِلَّا هُوَ ۖ فَأَنَّىٰ تُصْرَفُونَ
Ha-Mim. [These letters are one of the miracles of the Qur'an, and none but Allah (Alone) knows their meanings]. The revelation of the Book (this Qur'an) is from Allah, the All-Mighty, the All-Knower. The Forgiver of sin, the Acceptor of repentance, the Severe in punishment, the Bestower (of favours). La ilaha illa Huwa (none has the right to be worshipped but He), to Him is the final return. Surah Al-Ghafir 40:1-3	حم * تَنزِيلُ الْكِتَابِ مِنَ اللَّهِ الْعَزِيزِ الْعَلِيمِ *غَافِرِ الذَّنبِ وَقَابِلِ التَّوْبِ شَدِيدِ الْعِقَابِ ذِي الطَّوْلِ ۖ لَا إِلَهَ إِلَّا هُوَ ۖ إِلَيْهِ الْمَصِيرُ

That is Allah, your Lord, the Creator of all things: La ilaha illa Huwa (none has the right to be worshipped but He). How then are you turning away (from Allah, by worshipping others instead of Him)? Surah Al-Ghafir 40:62	ذَلِكُمُ اللَّهُ رَبُّكُمْ خَالِقُ كُلِّ شَيْءٍ لَا إِلَهَ إِلَّا هُوَ فَأَنَّى تُؤْفَكُونَ
He is the Ever Living, La ilaha illa Huwa (none has the right to be worshipped but He); so invoke Him making your worship pure for Him Alone (by worshipping Him Alone, and none else, and by doing righteous deeds sincerely for Allah's sake only, and not to show off, and not setting up rivals with Him in worship). All the praises and thanks be to Allah, the Lord of the 'Alamin (mankind, jinn and all that exists). Surah Al-Ghafir 40:65	هُوَ الْحَيُّ لَا إِلَهَ إِلَّا هُوَ فَادْعُوهُ مُخْلِصِينَ لَهُ الدِّينَ الْحَمْدُ لِلَّهِ رَبِّ الْعَالَمِينَ
La ilaha illa Huwa (none has the right to be worshipped but He). It is He Who gives life and causes death - your Lord and the Lord of your forefathers. Surah Ad-Dukhan 44:8	لَا إِلَهَ إِلَّا هُوَ يُحْيِي وَيُمِيتُ رَبُّكُمْ وَرَبُّ آبَائِكُمُ الْأَوَّلِينَ
He is Allah, beside Whom La ilaha illa Huwa (none has the right to be worshipped but He) the All-Knower of the unseen and the seen. He is the Most Gracious, the Most Merciful. Surah Al-Hashr 59:22	هُوَ اللَّهُ الَّذِي لَا إِلَهَ إِلَّا هُوَ عَالِمُ الْغَيْبِ وَالشَّهَادَةِ هُوَ الرَّحْمَنُ الرَّحِيمُ

He is Allah beside Whom La ilaha illa Huwa (none has the right to be worshipped but He), the King, the Holy, the One Free from all defects, the Giver of security, the Watcher over His creatures, the All-Mighty, the Compeller, the Supreme. Glory be to Allah! (High is He) above all that they associate as partners with Him. Surah Al-Hashr 59:23	هُوَ اللَّهُ الَّذِي لَا إِلَهَ إِلَّا هُوَ الْمَلِكُ الْقُدُّوسُ السَّلَامُ الْمُؤْمِنُ الْمُهَيْمِنُ الْعَزِيزُ الْجَبَّارُ الْمُتَكَبِّرُ ۚ سُبْحَانَ اللَّهِ عَمَّا يُشْرِكُونَ
Allah! La ilaha illa Huwa (none has the right to be worshipped but He). And in Allah (Alone) therefore, let the believers put their trust. Surah At-Taghabun 64:13	اللَّهُ لَا إِلَهَ إِلَّا هُوَ ۚ وَعَلَى اللَّهِ فَلْيَتَوَكَّلِ الْمُؤْمِنُونَ
(He Alone is) the Lord of the east and the west; La ilaha illa Huwa (none has the right to be worshipped but He). So take Him Alone as Wakil (Disposer of your affairs). Surah Al-Muzzammil 73:9	رَّبُّ الْمَشْرِقِ وَالْمَغْرِبِ لَا إِلَهَ إِلَّا هُوَ فَاتَّخِذْهُ وَكِيلًا

23 References

1. Quran

2. Hadith books

3. Zaad Al-MaAad by Ibn Al-Qayyim

4. Tafheem ul Quran by Maulana Syed Abul Ala Maududi

5. Jawame Dua, By: Khalid Aljuraisy

6. "Self Ruqyah Treatment" by Dr. K. Al-Jeraisy.

7. Attib un Nabawi" (Prophetic Medicine) by Ibn Al-Qayyim

8. Tafsir Ibn Kathir

9. Majmoo' Fataawa wa Maqaalaat Mutanawwiah by Al-Shaykh Al-Allaamah Abd Al-Azeez ibn Baaz

10. Majmoo' Fataawa Al-Shaykh Ibn Uthaymeen

11. Islamqa.info

12. IqraSense.com Online Blog

-- End --

24 Other Books by IqraSense

Note: These books are available at HilalPlaza.com

DUAs for Success (book) - 100+ Duas from Quran and Sunnah for success and happiness

- This book packs 100+ powerful DUAs that are effective for people in tough situations of life such as dealing with difficulties, financial issues, family, health issues, making tasks easy, success, and more.

- Includes AUTHENTIC DUAs from the Quran and Hadith (extracted from Saheeh Bukhari, Muslim, Abu Dawood, Tirmidhi, Ibn Maja, ...)

- Transform the way you make your DUAs by instead making the same DUAs using the same words that were used by the prophet (s)

- These DUAs are also recited by the Imams in Haram mosques in Makkah and Madinah during Taraweeh and Khatam Quran in Ramadan and other situations

- The book includes translation and transliteration of all the DUAs. Easy to memorize.

- The book provides potential uses for each DUA

- These DUAs provide us real solutions for when we need them the most

- The final chapter at the end includes the best of the best Duas as they are from the Quran with an explanation of when various prophets made those Duas to Allah.

DUAs in this book are suitable for asking Allah for:

- Relief from debts

- Increase in Rizq (provisions)

- Relief from anxiety and calmness in hearts

- Ease of difficulties

- Blessings for self and family

- Asking for righteous children

- Forgiveness of sins

- Staying firm in faith

- Asking for a sound character

- Asking for security for family

- High status in this life and the hereafter

- Refuge from calamities

- High status in Jannah

- Tawakkul (trust) in Allah

- Success in this life and the hereafter

- Health and wealth

- Asking for lawful provisions

- Protection from persecution

- Refuge from laziness and old age

- Relief from poverty

- Protection from Satan and other evils

- and 100+ more Duas

"The Power of Dua" - An Essential Guide to Increase the Effectiveness of Making Dua to Allah

This best selling Islamic book's goal is simply to provide information from Quran, Hadith, and Scholarly explanations / Quranic interpretations to increase the chances of Dua's getting accepted.

In this information packed publication, you will learn answers to these commonly asked questions:

- Why should we make dua when everything is already decreed?

- What can hold acceptance of Dua? (Important question)

- What can help make Duas accepted? (Important question)

- What should never be asked in a dua?

- A complete checklist that you can keep handy and work on as a reminder

- Can Dua be made in prayers?

- What mistakes do people make after duas are answered?

- What are the effects of Dhikr on making Dua? (very important)

- What role does Quran play in the acceptance of your Dua?

- What are the stipulations for acceptance of dua?

- Why making dua to Allah is not an option, but a necessity.

- Understanding the life transformational powers of Dua

- How dua CAN change what is already decreed?

- The benefits of making dua

- Allah's sayings with regard to dua

- What mistakes people make that make Dua's "suspended" rather than accepted?

- What are the mistakes related to the topic of Dua that makes Allah angry?

- What happens when a dua appears to be unanswered?

- What about the wait in getting Dua accepted?

- What are the times when Dua is accepted?

- Which people's Dua are especially accepted?

- What about the act of wiping one's face after making a Dua?

- What if someone asks Allah something that is sinful?

- How to Invoke Allah in Dua?

- What is the best position for Making Dua?

- What is the best place for making Dua?

- Dua's that various Prophets made for various situations, and difficulties that they faced

- and more....

Jesus - The Prophet Who Didn't Die

This book's goal is simply to provide information from Quran, Hadith, and Scholarly explanations / Quranic interpretations about the story of Jesus and the counter arguments in the Quran about Jesus, and other Christianity fundamentals.

The book will take you back in time and narrate Islamic viewpoints on the day of the crucifixion, the story of disciples of Jesus, Mary, Jesus's disciples and more - all from an Islamic standpoint. You will come to know about the Quranic verses that are specifically addressed to Christians about some of the claims of Christianity, Jesus, and more.

In this information packed book, you will learn the following:

- The story of the birth of Maryam (Mary) to her parents Imran and Hannah

- Maryam's (Mary's) mother promise to God (Allah)

- What Allah said about Maryam about her birth

- The story of the Rabbis, and Zakkariyyah in Bait Al-Maqdis in Jerusalem

- The story of the Jewish Rabbis' lottery about them competing to adopt Maryam

- The Hint from God (Allah) to Maryam about Jesus (Eesa's) birth

- Maryam's ordeal during and before Jesus's (Eesa's) birth

- The Quranic story about Maryam and the Angel that spoke to Maryam

- The birth of Jesus (Eesa) in Bethlehem as mentioned in the Quran

- Jesus speaking from the cradle in defense of Maryam (Mary)

- Ibn Kathir's depiction on how certain Jewish priests hid the birth of Maryam (Mary)

- Jesus's (Eesa's) teachings and how they parallel in the Quran and the Bible (Injeel)

- Ibn Kathir's story on Jesus's visit to the Jewish temple the night prophets John (pbuh) and Zakariyah (pbuh) died

- Islamic views on disciples of Jesus

- The story of Jesus's disciples in the Quran

- Islamic view on how the story of disciples in Christianity contradicts Biblical teachings and Quranic teachings

- Miracles of Jesus (Eesa) as described by Allah

- The story how Jesus (Eesa) was asked to prove his miracles

- How Angel Gabriel (Jibreel) supported Jesus (Eesa) to do miracles that many mistook as Jesus (Eesa's) miracles

- How Allah explicitly mentions that Jesus (being a human being) was granted some powers (through the Angel and others)

- A presentation about the strong affirmation in Quran on how Jesus (Eesa) was not crucified

- The Islamic story about how Jesus (Eesa) was convicted of crimes by certain Jewish priests of the time

- The Islamic story about how Jesus (Eesa) spoke to five of his companions about the crucifixion

- How Christian scripture too supports that Jesus was not God

- Quran's explanation in Quran about the Christian claims of making Jesus (Eesa) as son of God

- How Allah questions Jesus about him being worshipped by people

- The story about Jesus's (Eesa's) second coming in Islam

- The hadith about Jesus breaking the cross in his second coming

- Explanation on New Testament's contradictions about Jesus's (Eesa's) life

- and much more.......

Jerusalem is OURs - The Christian, Islamic, and Jewish struggle for the "Holy Lands"

"Jerusalem is Ours" is one of the first books that goes behind the scenes in history and delves into the religious underpinnings of the Abrahamic religions (Islam, Christianity, and Judaism) for their fervent support of Jerusalem and adjoining territories referred to as the Holy Lands by many.

Quoting the religious texts of Jews (Torah, Tanakh,Talmud), Christians (Bible), and Muslims (Quran and Hadith), this book provides a clear picture of why the Muslims, Jews, and Christians hold Jerusalem so close to their hearts. The quoted verses of the religious texts in Quran, Bible, and Torah will make you appreciate the religious significance of Jerusalem for the various faiths and the conflicts that has plagued that region for centuries.

The following are some of the topics covered in this book:

Torah / Talmud and Quranic verses and stories on Jerusalem

- World Zionist Organization - From "Holy Lands" to making of Israel

- Evangelical Christians in the United States and their Support for Israel

- Jesus in Jerusalem and the Islamic and Christian Stories of his crucifixion

- Popes of the 11th and 12th centuries and the Christian Crusader Attacks

- Concepts of "Greater Israel" and "Rebuilding of the Temple"

- Jerusalem during End of Times

- Holy Sites in Jerusalem

- Islamic Rule in Jerusalem

- Pre-historic Jerusalem

- and more...

ABOUT THE AUTHOR

IqraSense.com is a blog covering religion topics on Islam and other religious topics. To discuss this topic in more detail, you are encouraged to join the discussion and provide your comments by visiting the blog.

Made in the USA
Monee, IL
12 April 2024

56864381R00105